work your
assets off

work your
assets off

STOP WORKING SO HARD
IN BUSINESS AND IN LIFE

ALLISON TABOR

Published in the United States by Storyzon LLC.
www.storyzon.com

ISBN-13: 978-1-947480-66-7

FOREWORD

by Marshall Goldsmith

Peter Drucker taught me our mission in life is to make a positive difference, not to prove we're smart, not to prove we're right. Certainly not to prove how hard we can outwork people.

I agree with Allison Tabor when she points out that the first big lie in business is this: to get anywhere in life, you have to work hard.

We get so lost in proving we're smart and hardworking that we forget that's not why we're here on earth. We're here to make a positive difference, not to prove how smart we are, not to prove we can work harder than everybody else.

Instead, align your natural talents and your interests. Then you will experience success with greater ease.

My advice to achieve success with ease is to begin today to act like a businessperson but think like an artist. The most successful leaders know that building a masterpiece of a business and a life needs to start now. Not next week, not next year, and not when you decide on an encore retirement career, but right now.

Perhaps another word for masterpiece is *legacy,* which is often thought of as something left behind or handed down by a predecessor. While that may be true and common, what's not so commonly understood is that legacies do not appear upon retirement, departure, or death. Legacies are created daily.

There was a time when people thought new technology would lead to a life of ease. Instead, new technology has created a 24-7 mind-set. Professionals everywhere can be seen using smartphones to communicate with their coworkers. New technology has gone hand in hand with globalization to create a world where work never stops. It has also begun to blur the distinction between home and work.

Is this the case for you? I suggest you use this book as a wake-up call. In which areas might you need a little help? Make a checklist of behaviors and actions that you want to improve on and then ask someone to help you by listening to you gauge how you're doing every day.

Leveraging your assets is simple but still hard to do because we have to look at ourselves every single day. *Work Your ASSets Off* can be a great tool on this path. I wish you easeful success in business and in life.

Life is good!

Marshall Goldsmith is the *New York Times* #1 best-selling author of *Triggers, Mojo,* and *What Got You Here Won't Get You There.*

Work Your ASSets Off is filled with powerful insights and practical ideas about how to enjoy your business and life without having to work so hard.

—Marci Shimoff, *New York Times* #1 best-selling author of *Happy for No Reason* and *Chicken Soup for the Woman's Soul*

Work Your ASSets Off takes you to the deepest truth about your work life. It's not about how hard you work, it's about how much heart you work! Allison Tabor shows us how to enJOY both business and personal life and succeed!

—Dr. Brenda Wade, *Dr. Oz Show* relationship expert, best-selling author, and creator of the Modern Love Training

Through countless interactions with organizational leaders, Allison captures the singular essence of what the best leaders do differently to achieve stellar results. She then distills these lessons down into digestible, easily implementable action steps anyone can put to work in their company tomorrow! This book helps you understand that the old paradigm of blind hard work and killing yourself to succeed just isn't true . . . period. Allison pulls the curtain back to show you how the top-performing leaders really perform, and it's not how you think.

—Jay Niblick, founder/CEO of Innermetrix Inc. and best-selling author of *The Profitable Consultant* (foreword by Marshall Goldsmith) and *What's Your Genius?* (foreword by Tony Robbins)

Allison's strengths-based approach to work really works. Follow her principles and watch your business soar!

—MJ Ryan, author of *Attitudes of Gratitude* and *This Year I Will*

There are no straight lines in life or business! There are unexpected bumps and potholes offset by moments of unexpected joy. Wherever you are on your journey, Allison Tabor is going to help you rediscover who you are now and what's really important to you. *Work Your Assets Off* is an incredible handbook for how to move forward with all of who you are!

—Jim Horan, entrepreneur, Amazon best-selling author, CEO advisor, and president of the One Page Business Plan Company

CONTENTS/TRUTHS

For Gladys (Mom),
who serves in the self-assigned role
as the president of my fan club in perpetuity.
Love you more and forever.

"Everything is hard before it is easy."
Goethe

INTRODUCTION

PUSH YOURSELF, just work harder and harder, and get others to work harder too. Eventually, you will become successful and feel happier. Right?

No, not at all true.

Bookshelves are filled with countless self-improvement and business management books that promise a better life or business, if only you can learn how to work harder. Well, this book isn't one of them. In fact, I call BS on the idea that working harder translates into becoming more successful or happier.

So many of us go from college to cubicle to casket working hard and yet failing to find satisfaction. When we start to notice it's not working, we think we need to double down on our effort and work even harder. No pain, no gain, right? But rather than freeing ourselves from this vicious cycle, we get mired in it even deeper.

How many of us can honestly say that we feel energized, fulfilled, and "in the flow"? That we are living our best life?

The good news is that there is a way to break free from the cycle. We need to realize the difference between working our ***es off and working our ASSets off. Understanding this distinction will change your life.

This book was written for business owners, executives, and other individuals who are simply ready to stop working harder and harder. Join me on a journey to leverage your natural talents and start living your best life with ease. Let's get started with working our ASSets off!

truth #1

Truth #1: Working Your ASSets Off—Not Working Hard—Leads to Success

Lie #1: To get anywhere in life,
you have to work hard.

*"Working hard is important.
But what matters even more is to understand,
align, inspire, and apply yourself."*
—Allison Tabor

DO YOU EVER BRAG about how hard you work? Has anybody ever told you about how they pulled an all-nighter at work, as if it were a badge of honor?

Growing up, I was taught that a good work ethic was synonymous with long, hard work. And how hard we worked was tied not only to what good would come our way but also to how good a person we would become. The prediction was simple and straightforward. If something comes too easily, it is highly suspicious and probably nothing but a fleeting bubble of success. Lasting progress, by contrast, is forged from an iron will and must be earned with blood and sweat.

Because of this misconceived philosophy, we have today an epidemic of a "not good enough" mind-set afflicting countless people. Even those considered successful by most standards often suffer from frustration or depression due to a feeling of insufficiency and a sense that they need to do more.

As an executive coach, I've had the honor and privilege of working closely with some very accomplished business owners and executives. It took me by surprise to learn how many of them experience what I refer to as "imposter syndrome." Some feel insecure and question themselves when things seem to come too easily. They wonder if they were simply lucky and if their success was undeserved—in short, they often feel like imposters rather than truly successful people.

The truth is that most of these people were doing something right. Instead of just working themselves to the bone, they were working their ASSets off. This is a good thing, right? It is! But only if they can recognize, appreciate, and internalize this distinction. Doing so allows for greater achievements and deeper enjoyment of what they have accomplished. And of what they have!

A natural starting point for our exploration is to be aware of our own belief system. Do you tend to question things that come to you too easily? Do you feel you are more deserving if you had to work really hard? Do you sometimes hear the whispering of a "not good enough" voice? When you find yourself stuck, try to notice not only the external circumstances but also your own mind-set.

Conversely, there were likely times in which you were already working your ASSets off, when you were "in the zone," accomplishing what you set out to do with intuitive certainty and great ease—but you may not have even noticed! We need to learn to observe ourselves and recognize the difference between these opposite modalities, so we have the freedom to consciously choose and create our path forward.

Can you remember a job, project, or situation in which you were involved that seemed to really energize, excite, or satisfy you? Probably it was when you were aligned with your natural talents and interests.

While you can teach, motivate, and discipline yourself to achieve certain goals, doing so doesn't necessarily translate into being successful or feeling fulfilled. Rather, when you are aligned with your natural talents and interests, you will experience success with greater ease. Your potential expands as you leverage your ASSets.

Let's take a moment to consider the path that led you to where you are today. What made you choose your current career? Were you led to it through external circumstances? Maybe a family member, teacher, or mentor influenced or encouraged you. Or maybe your path was already laid out, as you are part of a multigenerational family business. Some people feel they were "predestined" or expected to fill certain roles, without even considering alignment with their own interests or natural talents.

Maybe you knew from an early age what you wanted to do in life. Maybe it was a progression of opportunities that happened to show up. Did you feel drawn to it, or did you resign yourself to it? Did you design your path or stumble into it?

In this early stage of self-investigation, it is crucial that you be honest with yourself. Understand and acknowledge the factors that shaped your path, free of all judgments. Whether your path came about by design, circumstance, or happenstance, it is what it is. BE HONEST about which it is.

After you've taken a moment to look at *why* you are where you are, let's now check in with *who* you are.

Have you ever taken an inventory of your ASSets? The ASSets of YOU, not what you own or invest in.

Let's fire up our brains! We want to assess *how* we are working and then examine if that reality lines up with our true ASSets.

This is a good time to take out a notebook, journal, or some writing paper.

Answer the following questions. Try not to skip any of them, and feel free to jot down anything and everything that comes to your mind.

1. What are you naturally good at?
2. What inspires you?
3. What have you been doing well easily versus what you have had to learn to do well?
4. What situations or opportunities energize you?
5. Under what circumstances are you at your best?
6. When do you feel most fully expressed?
7. What interests haven't you explored?

Answering these initial self-understanding questions is a big first step towards working your ASSets off.

These are questions that appear pretty simple and yet for most of us they will be hard to answer. Don't worry if you are not sure! We'll have more opportunities to meaningfully explore them as we go along.

Aside from your skills, what is the most important thing that you bring to any job or project? You bring *yourself*.

We each have our own interests, biases, communication styles, motivators, and experiential histories. Understanding these factors in conjunction with your transferable skills is a powerful combination that will propel you on your journey towards working your ASSets off.

Let's delve deeper to examine what these factors and skills are for you.

Once you have answered the initial set of self-reflection questions, you are ready for the questionnaire below. Your responses will illuminate where you fall on the continuum towards working your ASSets off. Let's redirect your energy with purpose!

Working Hard versus Working Your ASSets Off Assessment

Consider each of the following 25 statements and indicate whether it is:

- Not True (NT)
- Somewhat True (ST)
- Mostly True (MT)

Enjoyment/Fulfillment

1. I am good at what I do.
2. I enjoy the work I do.
3. I enjoy the people with whom I work.
4. I enjoy the environment in which I work.
5. My work is gratifying to me.
6. I feel inspired and energized in my work.

Self-Understanding

1. I understand what motivates me.
2. I am aware of my natural talents.
3. I am aware of my undeveloped talents or non-talents.
4. I have identified my personal values.
5. I know what gets in my way.

State/Mind-set

1. I feel successful in my work.
2. I feel confident in my abilities.
3. What I do matters to me and others.
4. I deserve to be successful and happy.
5. I have a positive outlook.
6. I feel grateful.

Leverage

1. I freely let others do things and don't feel like I have to do everything myself.

2. I work with ease.

3. I do what comes naturally to me.

4. My work feels aligned with my talents.

5. My work feels aligned with my interests.

6. I align myself with others who have complementary talents.

7 I leverage or even exploit my talents.

8. I encourage or lead others to align with their natural talents.

Look at what you jotted down. You may find that some of these statements are truer than others. Or that you see the need to dig deep here, understand what makes you tick, and consider changing some things up.

You have an opportunity to live and work with more grace and ease. By reading this book and embracing the knowledge and truths herein, you'll find it simpler to ease your way through work and life! Ready? Let's get going.

"Your work is going to fill a large part of your life, and the only way to be truly satisfied is to do what you believe is great work. And the only way to do great work is to love what you do. If you haven't found it yet, keep looking. Don't settle. As with all matters of the heart, you'll know when you find it."
—Steve Jobs

truth #2

Truth #2: It's Better to Be Great at Being You Than to Be Good at Everything

Lie #2: To get anywhere in life,
you have to be good at everything.

*"The difference between stupidity and genius
is that genius has its limits."*
—Albert Einstein

*"I want you to be everything that's you,
deep at the center of your being."*
—Confucius

BUSINESS OWNERS DON'T ALWAYS HAVE IT EASY. At times, it can feel like a wild rollercoaster ride with ups, downs, and unexpected sharp turns. Entrepreneurs often wear many hats and face real setbacks, including partner disputes; attracting, managing, and keeping quality employees and clients; thriving in a competitive environment; managing cash flow and profitability; and fighting off competition. All of this must be handled while maintaining compliance with ever-changing laws and regulations. Then, underneath the stress, is the pressure— pressure to succeed, rather than become a business failure statistic. According to data from the Bureau of Labor Statistics, about 20% of small businesses fail in their first year, and about 50% by their fifth year. Scary stuff.

For some entrepreneurs, stress translates into depression. Recently, a few seemingly "successful" and iconic entrepreneurs committed suicide. It came as a shock to many of us when we learned that fashion designer Kate Spade and celebrity chef Anthony Bourdain had taken their own lives. By most standards, they seemed to be "living the dream." But it can be a dream with a high price tag. Notwithstanding their personal status or business success, 30% of all entrepreneurs experience depression, according to a study by Dr. Michael Freeman, a clinical professor at the University of California, San Francisco. Given the stigma often associated with the subject of depression, the actual numbers are perhaps even higher.

In addition to contributing to depression, business stress can also strain interpersonal relationships. About 90% of all U.S. businesses are family-owned or controlled by a family. Family-owned businesses face not only the usual business-related challenges but also have the added difficulty of family dynamics. The stakes seem higher due to greater personal entanglement. There might be resentment associated with some family members seemingly taking advantage of others; unequal effort versus rewards between family members; blurry boundaries between work and personal life; and more.

Imagine the Thanksgiving dinner experience. Can people who work together relate as a family without the conversation being consumed by business? If they have business frustrations with each other, will it seep into their personal relationships? Without addressing the potential challenges, these dynamics can be unnecessarily hard.

In addition to those concerns, such coworkers may feel the added pressure of keeping the family legacy going, given that less than one-third of family businesses survive the transition from first- to second-generation ownership, and another 50% don't survive the transition from second- to third-generation ownership. Each of these circumstances ups the temperature of the pressure cooker.

It should come as no surprise that business owners commonly experience disengagement, stress, isolation, frustration, and burnout. These feelings have presented so often among my clients and colleagues that I now consider them to be symptoms of a larger "dissatisfaction epidemic" among business owners.

Not only have I seen this with others, but I've experienced periods of stress and burnout during various stages of my own career. Fortunately I have discovered some amazing keys to avoid the pitfalls and engage in best practices for success. Throughout our journey together, I will share these with you.

So where does all of the pressure begin? Often, in the early phases of a new business, owners are faced with limited resources. They may be unable to afford qualified personnel or necessary business tools, and so they learn to manage—and sometimes even master—many different aspects of their businesses themselves. The owners become the chief bottle washers, doing just about everything. Sound familiar?

While this approach is most prevalent in the start-up phase, it also carries forward into later stages of business development. Many business owners will try to learn as much as they can about everything. The more complex the business, the thinner they will spread themselves. Of course, it *is* helpful to have a basic understanding of all things relevant to your business, but what these owners fail to see is the distinction between having a good basic understanding of operations and trying to be an expert at everything. While the former is a necessity, the latter is a disservice to the business and to themselves.

There are three underlying problems with trying to be master of all things:

1: In order to scale a business, you must rely on others, not simply on yourself. A must-read book for every business owner that addresses this very subject is *The E-Myth Revisited* by Michael Gerber. Gerber delivers a dose of reality to business owners, distinguishing between those who truly have a business and those who have a self-created job.

2: Trying to personally do everything that needs to be done will likely result in disengagement, stress, frustration, burnout, lost opportunity, and eventually, business failure. These feelings will magnify not only for you but for your employees as well.

3: You can't possibly be great at everything you do! Is this possibly an ego issue? A trust issue? A denial issue? Only for you to explore and address.

Often my clients recognize that there is a problem, but they don't necessarily know what to do about it. This is what I tell them:

Embrace your suck and focus on your strengths!

Most of us are uncomfortable embracing our weaknesses. We tend to deny them, eliminate them, or work on them until they are no longer considered weaknesses. In other words, we focus on fixing what is weak.

This "fixing" approach is made easier through the use of technology, which enables us to educate ourselves about almost anything by simply googling it, watching a YouTube video, or taking an online course. But this method is fatally flawed. While I too appreciate the easy access to information, it doesn't mean that we have suddenly developed an unlimited capacity for learning. Most of us are in constant danger of information overload. When we focus on fixing our weaknesses, we are playing a hand we can never win. We simply cannot be experts at everything.

Rather than constantly trying to fix ourselves, we should ask, What do I suck at? And then accept it, manage it, and maneuver through your situation to accommodate for it.

We do this by *developing and leveraging our strengths.* Focusing on our strengths rather than our shortcomings will pay much greater dividends.

As best-selling author of *Secrets of the Millionaire Mind*, T. Harv Eker, said, "Where attention goes, energy flows and results show."

Where attention goes, energy flows! So why not place your attention on what you want to create or experience naturally and easily?

Where has your attention been going? Have you found yourself focusing on what you think you need to do, rather than what you're excited about and drawn to do? What pops up as being in natural alignment with your talents?

When I started placing my own attention on what I wanted, liked, and was good at, more of those opportunities started to appear. Perhaps some of them were there all along and went unnoticed. Seeing opportunities through the lens of alignment was expansive. The more aligned I was, the more gratified and effective I was; my desired results multiplied. While I am a big proponent of intentional strategic planning, I also discovered the importance of intentional thinking. We'll dive further into the topic of intentional thinking later on our journey.

Once you recognize and understand your natural talents, your expertise will develop within that particular area or discipline. If you want to develop expertise in certain areas, start by mastering your self-awareness!

CASE STUDY

I once worked with a 48-person therapeutic service business that was owned and managed by two partners who were best friends from college. Let's call them Claire and Lisa. Also helping to manage the business was Lisa's husband, Peter.

All three were overwhelmed and unable to keep up with the growth of their business. They felt that they were out of control and that they were run by the business rather than running it. With so much at stake, they were committed to becoming better owners and leaders.

During a process of inquiry, it was revealed that they didn't have defined roles and responsibilities among themselves. When asked who the acting CEO was, they said that they shared the role. They were collectively responding to the needs of the business and "sharing the role and load," as they described it. This lack of clear definition in their roles and responsibilities not only left each of them misaligned with their natural strengths and talents but it also left the company without clear leadership.

So we created an organizational chart based on the company's needs and then turned our attention to exploring their different abilities, interests, and objectives to match them to the needed roles.

Through various assessments and our interpretive discussions, it soon became obvious which roles and responsibilities were in alignment with their individual and collective ASSets. This helped inform a new leadership team structure. We also identified areas of needed expertise that were not covered by their skills, and we found key employees with those skills to join their management team.

This shifted their approach from "we can share and do anything as needed" to one that identified and aligned the business owners and team members with their collective strengths. Rather than trying to be experts at everything, they began to work their ASSets off.

Over the course of several months, we applied the same methodology to other areas of their business—all based on the principle of focusing and leveraging their strengths rather than trying to compensate for their weaknesses. They acknowledged that they had been "on a hamster wheel," constantly reacting to their circumstances. Their sense of being overwhelmed was replaced with purpose, focus, and security. Today, they continue to lead by leveraging their ASSets.

truth #3

Truth #3: The "F" Word—Focus—It Is Essential to Focus On Cultivating Unique Strengths

Lie #3: The "F" word is bad.

"Do not let what you cannot do interfere with what you can do."
—John Wooden, basketball player and former head coach at UCLA

AS IMPRACTICAL AS IT IS to try to turn our weaknesses into strengths, the idea that we should do just that is a widely held belief.

A great number of self-help books suggest that we should focus on what we could do better and improve upon our weaknesses until they become our strengths. Well intended as this advice may be, it has contributed to many people feeling constantly inadequate, "not enough." And to compensate for this feeling of insufficiency, they work harder and harder to dig out of a self-made hole.

As Albert Einstein pointed out, "Everybody is a genius. But if you judge a fish for its ability to climb a tree, it will live its whole life believing it is stupid." This not only applies to judging others, but the same principle applies to self-judgment. Think about it. Is it at all reasonable to judge ourselves for being poor tree climbers if we have gills and are meant to swim? Of course not! However, we often judge ourselves and others simply for not being exceptional at things we aren't naturally designed for.

Where does this unrealistic expectation come from? A culture of expecting fish to climb trees can be traced to childhood. Some may have experienced this at home, and it certainly was prevalent in our education system growing up. In schools, the focus was, and still is, deficit based, rather than based on harnessing each student's unique strengths. Most students weren't acknowledged or valued for their strengths but rather graded against a standard of expected performance.

In a TED talk with over 57 million views, *Do Schools Kill Creativity* author Sir Ken Robinson challenges the way we're educating our children, championing "a radical rethink of our school systems, to cultivate creativity and acknowledge multiple types of intelligence."

Fast-forward to adulthood, and the "not enough" feeling has become a pandemic. This truth became evident to me over ten years ago when I attended a conference designed for entrepreneurs. Over a thousand attendees were invited to write a self-limiting belief on one side of a thick plywood board, and a desired state of mind on the other. Then we participated in an exercise, at the end of which we were asked to break the board with our bare hands. Doing so, we were told, symbolized breaking though our limiting beliefs and making our desired states possible.

Two things made this day remarkable for me. For one, I was amazed at how everyone, with no martial arts training, was able to break the thick boards.

As incredible as that was, however, something else struck me even more. Before breaking our boards, we were asked to hold them up and walk around, so that everybody could see them. What blew me away was that the vast majority of the boards showed the same theme, the same self-limiting belief, of being "not enough." Wow, I thought. How could so many "successful people" possibly not feel they were good enough, young enough, rich enough, smart enough, or fast enough? You fill in the blank.

Fast-forward further to today, and the same mind-set prevails, perhaps to an even larger degree. In working closely with business owners and executives, I see firsthand how many of them experience what I referred to earlier as the "imposter syndrome," a variation of the "not enough" mentality. Many of these business leaders are very successful, and yet they suffer from feeling deficient.

This begs the question, what is enough? When are *we* enough? And what if, instead of working on our weaknesses, we embraced our suck and leveraged our strengths? Imagine if we shifted our focus away from not being enough? What if, instead, we focused on how we already *are* enough?

Recently, I viewed a thought-provoking TEDx talk, "How to Make the Most Out of Not Having Enough," by Kelly Goldsmith. Goldsmith said, "Today, people regularly feel like they don't have enough—not enough time, not enough money, not enough followers on Instagram. Can these everyday experiences of scarcity actually have positive consequences?"

Goldsmith speaks to when we feel we don't *have* enough. However, what if we apply her point to those people who experience *feeling* not-enough? Perhaps feeling that way serves as motivation to keep doing more for our businesses, community, and the world.

By now, I hope you can see there is a better way than just working hard.

Can you think of times when you felt you were "in the zone"? When everything seemed just right and you felt good, really good? Maybe your adrenaline was rushing, and you felt pumped, or maybe you experienced a sense of calm and peace. Whatever your personal experience, you may have recognized that zone moment as being different from other times, when perhaps you didn't feel particularly comfortable, capable, interested, or empowered, let alone unstoppable. When you experience being in your zone, everything seems to flow, everything feels right. You are focused—*you are enough!*

Sometimes we are easily able to identify why we are in the state of flow. When we can identify why, it is easier to become intentional. We can deliberately re-create the experiences that put us in this positive state.

There are usually clues, and if we just pause and pay attention, we will notice them. The key is to turn our attention towards finding common "themes." Often, that's easier when we don't focus on the specifics of a given situation but rather on what general elements and conditions are present that shift us into feeling we are in our zone.

When we pay close attention, we will notice that these conditions naturally align with our personal styles, interests, and talents. We are at our best when all of these factors are in sync.

Besides our unique styles, interests, and talents, there is yet another factor that determines if we are truly in our flow. This other half of the "in the zone" equation is tied to our core values. Most of our interests and behaviors are rooted in a set of core values, so when situations and circumstances align with these values, we propel ourselves forward into our zone.

I can't stress enough how important this value alignment is to your success. For a business owner, not only does it personally energize you but it also lets prospective customers and employees know where you stand. You will attract and retain the *right* customers and team members by working your ASSets off together.

A client had this to share about how their values connect their team members: *"We have various properties in different locations. Each hotel has its own unique considerations and identity, responsive to our varying customer needs. The significance of our Core Values is that they provide a consistent 'way of being' for our RH team, no matter which property. Further, our shared Core Values translate through to the client experience, no matter which hotel. We can say, they unite us to what matters."* —Sima Patel, CEO, Ridgemont Hospitality

IDEALLY, WE SHOULD ALL hire, fire, review, and reward employees and clients according to our core values.

Jerry I. Porras, Lane Professor Emeritus of Organizational Behavior and Change at Stanford University Graduate School of Business and coauthor of the 1994 bestseller *Success Built to Last: Creating a Life That Matters,* shared that "Companies that enjoy enduring success have core values and a core purpose that remain fixed, while their business strategies and practices endlessly adapt to a changing world. The dynamic of preserving the core while stimulating progress is the reason that companies such as Hewlett-Packard, 3M, Johnson & Johnson, Procter & Gamble, Merck, Sony, Motorola, and Nordstrom became elite institutions able to renew themselves and achieve super long-term performance."

When we intentionally surround ourselves with people who are aligned with our core values, we are more likely to create the kind of environment that has the entire team operating in the zone. Rather than working against an adversarial environment, we are now creating one that is mutually beneficial, where each person involved can respond naturally to situations and challenges. Everyone can work his or her ASSets off.

According to Tony Hsieh, CEO of Zappos, "Your personal core values define who you are, and a company's core values ultimately define the company's character and brand. For individuals, character is destiny. For organizations, culture is destiny."

Further, Robert T. Kiyosaki, author of *Rich Dad, Poor Dad*, said, "Inside every great brand is the DNA of the entrepreneur who started it all. That DNA is a precious and valuable asset that few companies even recognize they have until it is lost. If the DNA is not protected, the brand soon dies. This is why so many brands die when the entrepreneur sells their business to a big corporation."

Apple has been listed by *Forbes* as the most valuable business brand in the world, valued at $182.8 billion. Would it surprise you to know that the world's most valuable and iconic brand has an unwavering belief in its core values? As Apple founder Steve Jobs said, "When I thought deeply about this, I ended up concluding that the worst thing that could possibly happen as we get big and as we get a little more influence in the world is if we change our core values and start letting them slide. I can't do that. I'd rather quit."

Here are the seven core values of Apple, which form the company's corporate culture:

1. *We believe that we're on the face of the Earth to make great products that will change the world.*
2. *We believe in the simple, not the complex.*
3. *We believe that we need to own and control the primary technologies behind the products we make.*
4. *We participate only in markets where we can make a significant contribution.*
5. *We believe in saying no to thousands of projects so that we can really focus on the few that are truly important and meaningful to us.*
6. *We believe in deep collaboration and cross-pollination of our groups, which allow us to innovate in a way that others cannot.*
7. *We don't settle for anything less than excellence in every group in the company, and we have the self-honesty to admit when we're wrong and the courage to change.*

These core values became the DNA of the company. The Apple brand was built from this DNA.

The marketing strategy of Apple is based on the core values of the company. Product development, promotion, distribution, customer service, and all other functions of the company are informed by its core values!

Why didn't the brand die when Steve Jobs died in 2011? Because Tim Cook, the current CEO of Apple, brilliantly recognized the critical importance of maintaining the core values from which Steve Jobs built the company. People continue to buy Apple products because of their affinity to the brand. They love and believe in the brand.

LET'S TAKE A LOOK AT another business giant whose DNA remains in its core values, long after the passing of the founder.

The Walt Disney Company was founded by Walt Disney, along with his brother, Roy Disney. Walt Disney, considered to be one of the most prominent cultural icons of all time, was an animator, cartoonist, entrepreneur, and film producer. By the time of his death in 1966, he left behind a lasting legacy.

> The Walt Disney Family Museum is an American museum that explores the life and legacy of Walt Disney. The museum is located in the Presidio of San Francisco, part of the Golden Gate National Recreation Area in San Francisco. It offers a fascinating glimpse into the business story and the life of a visionary business owner who was faced with many challenges. I found that the exhibit offered business owners a peek into real and relatable experiences, lessons learned, and clues that contributed to Disney's success.

Having clear core values is also key to sound personal decision-making. In fact, whenever we are faced with a decision of some importance, we should pause and consider our values. Decisions tend to become easier when they are processed through the filter of what really matters to us.

Your core values inform your thoughts, words, and actions.

Recently, I had a client experience that illustrated this well. An architect coaching client was updating his website and felt frustrated with his website designer. Having helped my client and his team to articulate their core values, I was familiar with them and recognized right away that the website designer was clashing with those values.

Let's peek into the situation, starting with a look at my client's core values.

Architect's Core Values

COMMITTED
We take personal responsibility to provide excellent work, respond to the needs of our clients, and deliver quality design.

DESIGN MATTERS
We seek creative design solutions that reflect our aesthetic principles.

COLLABORATIVE
Our collaborative process provides a thorough approach to our design solutions and promotes high-quality work.

PROBLEM-SOLVERS
We recognize problems, develop responsive solutions, and work together toward creative outcomes.

FUN
Our fun work environment breeds creativity and energizes us.

WHEN THE WEBSITE DESIGNER revealed his initial design, my client was underwhelmed. Recognizing the architect's disappointment, the website designer responded that while the back-end functionality of the proposed website was 80% complete, the design portion was only 20% complete.

His approach and presentation was completely dismissive of my client's core value:

DESIGN MATTERS
We seek creative design solutions that reflect our aesthetic values.

Why did the designer spend the majority of his time on the back-end functionality of the site? In doing so, he missed the obvious mark. My client had a strong appetite for creative design, which the website designer hadn't paid attention to.

The experienced website designer had the technical skill set to get the project done. However, his credibility and trust were compromised by his not taking into account what mattered most to my client.

My client decided to forfeit his 50% deposit and stop working with the website designer. What happened next triggered a conflict with my own core values! The website designer tried to pressure my client, insisting that he had a contractual obligation to complete the website and expected his full payment. His self-serving perspective antagonized the situation, and me. I stepped in to help my client, and the designer ultimately agreed to back down. Why did it bother me as much as it did my client? Because it conflicted with my own principles. Not only did the web designer's approach disregard my client's priorities and values, his treatment of my client was out of alignment with certain of my core values, such as generosity. He was not exemplifying either of these qualities. When my client invited my input and assistance with this, I supported his decision to cut bait. No matter the website designer's qualifications, there was a misalignment of core values.

Since we all see the world through the lens of our own core values, one might think that we would intrinsically know what they are. The truth is, most of our perceptions tend to be filtered through unconscious or semiconscious beliefs. It takes some work to cut through these beliefs and uncover our values. While simple, it's far from easy. So before introducing you to some resources that will help you clarify your core values, I have a few primers to get you started.

Ask yourself the following questions:

1. What matters most?
2. Who would you clone and what characteristics do they embody?
3. Who hasn't worked out in your company, and what undesirable characteristics did they exhibit?
4. How are you showing up? Are you walking your talk?
5. Are your core values aspirational or actual?

Take a close look at your answers. Can you begin to identify and write down your personal core values as they relate to you? What about your business's core values? Is there any overlap? There certainly should be, if it's your business!

Now that we've thought about what types of circumstances help us get into our zone and also looked at the core values we need for alignment, let's turn our attention to our skills and natural talents. As with our core values, we may know what our skills and talents are, but it is also possible that they are yet to be discovered.

A great resource to help us do this is an exercise from the classic book *What Color Is Your Parachute?* by Richard N. Bolles. Millions of copies of Bolles's book have been sold, and it is considered the most popular job-hunting book in the world. It was written not only for job hunters but also career changers. Bolles encouraged readers to "always define WHAT you want to do with your life and WHAT you have to offer to the world, in terms of your favorite talents/gifts/skills—not in terms of a job title."

I assert that Bolles's ideas are helpful beyond those who are looking for new work. I believe the same thoughtful inventory can benefit anyone who is ready to stop working so hard!

One section of his book is devoted to "Finding a Life…The Flower Exercise." Included are introspective exercises that help you to design what is described as "The Flower—That One Piece of Paper."

Bolles uses a process of brief story writing and analysis meant to help you discover your transferable skills, patterns, and priorities.

After I spent twenty-three years running a successful engineering business with my husband, I read Bolles's book and did the Flower Exercise. It turned out to be an important step in my professional transformation journey.

Even if we believe that we already understand ourselves, this exercise is helpful. While I knew myself pretty well to begin with, the exercises from the book helped me deepen my understanding and bring the information into super sharp focus. That information helped me make decisions that catapulted me into my zone. I am still here years later!

One of my favorite exercises in the book explores answers to the following questions:

1. *Who am I?*
2. *What turns me on about each of these?*
3. *Are there any common denominators?*
4. *What must my career use (and include) for me to be truly happy, useful, and effective?*

As part of Bolles's exercises, you are invited to write several stories (one short paragraph per story) to uncover transferable skills. Ultimately, the exercises lead you towards creating your "Flower—That One Piece of Paper."

Each petal of the flower represents an area of importance:

- *Favorite Interests*
- *Geography*
- *Favorite People*
- *Favorite Environment*
- *Favorite Values*
- *Favorite Working Conditions*
- *Salary and Level of Responsibility*
- *Favorite Skills* (prioritized and is the center of the flower)

Creating my "flower" was validating and insightful; it provided me with my own unique GPS coordinates towards success. As it turned out, these coordinates put me on a journey that culminated in a radical career change.

After twenty-three years of owning and running our structural engineering business, my husband and I exited our business to start our next chapter—together in life but separate in business. I had been coaching some of my colleagues for years before acknowledging it as such and "formalizing" it.

My "flower" revealed to me that many of my transferable skills, special knowledge, and values had been in play but had not taken center stage.

In 2009, I started my new career as a business coach and management consultant. This shift allowed me to focus on all my strengths while sprinkling in some of the additional insights gained, such as knowing the people and organizations with whom I wanted to work and the difference I wanted to make. I am not sure that without the Flower Exercise I would have discovered my new path quite so quickly.

So let's go back to the "Who am I?" question. It may be helpful for you to see the notes I scribbled down in response to the questions. Sharing my answers with you feels very personal to me, and I am afraid they may sound boastful or arrogant. However, I am a fan of *New York Times* best-selling author Brené Brown and her work on courage and vulnerability. Most importantly, I think there is value in your seeing just how this exercise connected me to what I do today, with the hope that it can create the same empowering opportunity for you, if you are ready to create your own flower.

Here are my actual "Who am I?" responses, leading up to the Flower Exercise, which follows:

#1 Who Am I
A Communicator

Why
Because I am articulate and love to engage with others.

What Turns Me On About This Is...
I am gratified when I am able to effectively communicate with others. I feel fully expressed.

#2 Who Am I
Balance Driven

Why
Because I need and thrive on having a healthy life balance.

What Turns Me On About This Is...
That I am able to live a multidimensional life that incorporates many areas of interest and importance to me. Sometimes simultaneously. This includes spending time with my spouse, family and friends, time for

myself, for exercise, spirituality and other interests. It is important for me to not only be successful in business but also to be a successful wife, mother, daughter, friend, and individual.

#3 Who Am I
A Connector

Why
Because I am always connecting people and listening for matchmaking opportunities in business and in life.

What Turns Me On About This Is...
That I have a rich network of diverse people, that I can connect with a wide variety of people, and that I am able to connect them to each other, creating win-win outcomes.

#4 Who Am I
A Compassionate Person

Why
Because I care deeply about people and things.

What Turns Me On About This Is...
That I am in touch with my feelings of care and empathy for others, making me feel human and connected.

#5 Who Am I
A Passionate Person

Why
Because I do many things with a great deal of conviction and passion.

What Turns Me On About This Is...
That when I believe in something or someone, I become fully immersed, inspired, committed, advocating, and supportive.

#6 Who Am I
An Entrepreneur

Why
Because I like being my own boss. I also like to lead myself and others.

What Turns Me On About This Is...
I love the challenging variety of activities, organizing and orchestrating, problem solving, strategizing, trusting my instincts, etc., associated with being a business owner. I am enterprising and resourceful.

#7 Who Am I
A Negotiator

Why
This connects to my being passionate. I am a person of conviction and I don't like the word no. I usually like the challenge of negotiating too. It is validating when my credibility carries through in a negotiation.

What Turns Me On About This Is...
I feel a sense of confidence when I'm negotiating for something I believe in, and I'm especially proud when I achieve the desired results. I have a strong sense of conviction. I am very credible and persuasive when I believe in a purpose, cause, etc.

#8 Who Am I
An Efficient Person

Why
Because I enjoy finding smarter, better, faster, easier ways of doing things. I have a pragmatic perspective. Wasted time or energy is disappointing.

What Turns Me On About This Is...
Knowing that I am good at recognizing and identifying opportunities for improvement. It feels good to get more out of things. It feels good to identify, create, or direct systems and procedures that promote efficiency.

#9 Who Am I
An Orchestrator

Why
I like to coordinate, control, and affect the outcome of situations.

What Turns Me On About This Is...
That I am able to effectively organize, lead, communicate, execute, and influence outcomes. I feel productive, effective, and useful when doing so.

#10 Who Am I
A Mentor

Why
It has been one of the most rewarding aspects of my career and community service.

What Turns Me On About This Is...
It feels great when I am able to inspire others and be inspired as well. It is very gratifying to make a difference through others.

Together, the "Who am I?" answers and my seven stories were used to determine my transferable skills and create my core flower. My flower brought into focus what mattered to me. It then became a road map and decision-making tool.

Using These **Transferable Skills:**
1. *Beginning new tasks, ideas, and projects*
2. *Negotiating, persuading*
3. *Talking or speaking with others*
4. *Following through on plans*
5. *Acting on gut reactions*

Flower Petal #1: Addresses geography

Flower Petal #2: Using these elements of special knowledge
- *Relationship building*
- *Facilitation*
- *Coordination*

Flower Petal #3: People environment
- *Enterprising*
- *Social*
- *Conventional*

Flower Petal #4: Goals/purpose/values
- *Able to demonstrate compassion for others*
- *Justice and fairness preside*
- *Human spirit is present through compassion and love*

Flower Petal #5: Addresses working conditions

Flower Petal #6: Addresses level of responsibility and salary

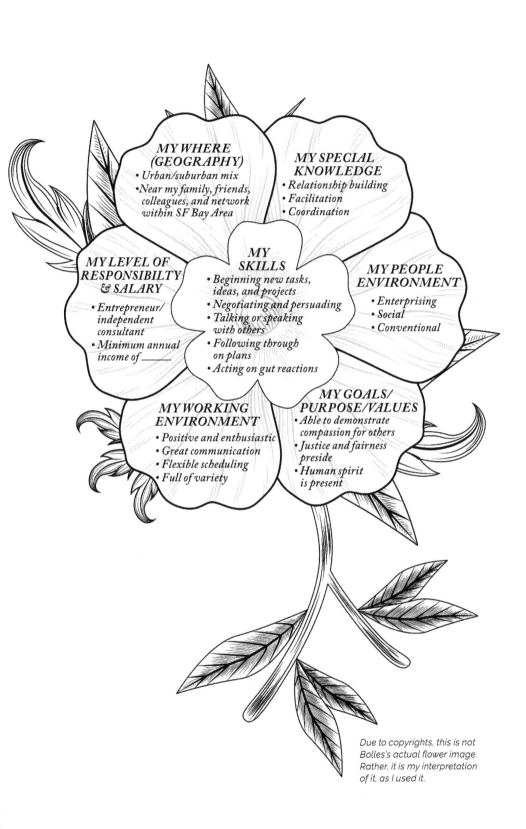

MY WHERE (GEOGRAPHY)
• Urban/suburban mix
• Near my family, friends, colleagues, and network within SF Bay Area

MY SPECIAL KNOWLEDGE
• Relationship building
• Facilitation
• Coordination

MY LEVEL OF RESPONSIBILTY & SALARY
• Entrepreneur/ independent consultant
• Minimum annual income of _____

MY SKILLS
• Beginning new tasks, ideas, and projects
• Negotiating and persuading
• Talking or speaking with others
• Following through on plans
• Acting on gut reactions

MY PEOPLE ENVIRONMENT
• Enterprising
• Social
• Conventional

MY WORKING ENVIRONMENT
• Positive and enthusiastic
• Great communication
• Flexible scheduling
• Full of variety

MY GOALS/ PURPOSE/VALUES
• Able to demonstrate compassion for others
• Justice and fairness preside
• Human spirit is present

Due to copyrights, this is not Bolles's actual flower image. Rather, it is my interpretation of it, as I used it.

My flower blooms!

Soon after completing this exercise, a colleague approached me with the news that she was resigning from her position as a facilitator with the Women Presidents' Organization (WPO). She suggested that I would be a perfect candidate for the consulting position, and she offered to recommend me, if I was interested.

I learned that the WPO was then made up of almost 1,600 CEOs of multimillion-dollar entrepreneurial enterprises who met in 100 professionally facilitated peer groups around the world. At the time, they had seventy-one "Chapter Chairs" and were seeking an independent consultant to facilitate a San Francisco East Bay Chapter. The WPO has continued to grow since. As of 2019, the organization has 141 chapters and 2,000 members worldwide!

I was happy to be introduced to the WPO and invited to interview for the position. They provided me with detailed information about the organization and position, including their vision, philosophy, characteristics, roles and responsibilities, and job description. Using my Flower Exercise notes, I compared the WPO opportunity to what I had discovered earlier about myself, and as I reviewed all of the information, I felt as if the role was custom designed for me! It was as subtle as a lightning bolt. While I'd started with a good sense of self-understanding, the Flower Exercise had projected a light onto my individual and collective experiences, preferences, and values. It had also become a checklist that I used as I considered the opportunity with the WPO.

Needless to say, I jumped on the opportunity and accepted the invitation. I was now in the fast lane on my journey towards working my ASSets off!

I am happy to report that this year, 2019, I celebrate my seventh year as a WPO facilitator, now with two thriving chapters. I love what I do, with whom I do it, what we accomplish together, and frankly, just being part of an incredible community of women leaders who make a difference all over the world.

Now professionally, I am enjoying both my coaching/management consulting business and my WPO facilitation role. They are very complementary, and both allow me to work my ASSets off! I am grateful for how aligned my life and career are with my blooming Flower. This too can be around the corner for you!

I hope that by openly sharing my detailed example, I reveal what can happen when you **identify and leverage your natural interests and talents.**

As you go about identifying and leveraging your natural interests and talents, you will recognize opportunities that align, allowing you to get into the flow and work your ASSets off.

> *"Working hard for something we don't care about is called stress. Working hard for something we love is called passion."*
> —Simon Sinek, author and motivational speaker

truth #4

Truth #4: People Want to Be Treated How *They* Want to Be Treated, Not the Way *You* Want to Be Treated

Lie #4: You should treat others the way you want to be treated.

"Do unto others as they would want done to them."
—Dave Kerpen, author of *The Art of People*

NOW THAT WE'VE SHARPENED our focus regarding our own natural interests and talents, we may begin to broaden our view by considering those around us. Seems simple enough, right? The challenge, however, is that we tend to view others and the world through our own unique lens. This is particularly obvious when it comes to our ideas about how a person wants to be treated.

Working our ASSets off includes finding the key to working with others' needs.

"Treat others the way you want to be treated" is known as the Golden Rule. It is a well-intended, highly extolled virtue meant to remind us to be considerate members of the community. Adopting this belief can cause unintended negative consequences, however, because we practice it quite literally—through our biased lens of what we expect ideal treatment looks like.

Have you ever had a conversation with someone that didn't turn out as well as you anticipated, even though you had the best of intentions? Have you been completely stumped or disappointed by someone's reaction to what you felt was a thoughtful and caring way of approaching them or a problem?

That is because people don't want to be treated the way *you* want to be treated; rather, they want to be treated the way *they* want to be treated.

Dave Kerpen, in *The Art of People*, asserts that the Golden Rule has things all wrong. He suggests we should instead follow what he calls the Platinum Rule: "We all grow up learning about the simplicity and power of the Golden Rule: Do unto others as you would want done to you. It's a splendid concept except for one thing: Everyone is different, and the truth is that in many cases what you'd want done to you is different from what your partner, employee, customer, investor, spouse, family member, friend, or even a stranger would want done to them."

Kerpen's Platinum Rule takes into account that all people and situations are different. If you follow the rule, you can assure yourself a better outcome. The key is to understand that we humans are unique and that each of us has our own perspective influenced by our experiences, values, motivators, and preferred communication styles.

Do you ever think, if only everyone were just like me?

Of course not, you say? Well, our behavior suggests the contrary. After all, we are most comfortable with people who are like us. We often surround ourselves with people who behave most like us. It's easier, right? And when we interact with people who aren't just like us, we frequently think, "What's wrong with them?!" Nothing is wrong; actually, their ASSets are simply different. So rather than trying to force them into a mold that looks more like ours, it is better to try and understand their preferences (and how they differ from our own), so that everyone can work their ASSets off together!

There are a great number of tools and resources available to help you accomplish this. One of my favorites is the highly validated DISC communication style assessment.

I first used DISC in my engineering business. It was a great communication and team-building tool that helped me with my staff of engineers, drafters, and administrative employees. It transformed our communication and performance, both individually and collectively, as evidenced by tangible bottom-line results.

This was the catalyst that led to my using DISC and other behavioral assessments while coaching others to produce extraordinary results. Leveraging behavioral analytic tools in business and life is another example of how I began to work my ASSets off and then helped others do the same.

So, what is DISC anyway?

DISC is a popular and effective communication tool based on behavioral research by William Moulton Marston, which dates back to 1928. Over time, it has become the universal language of human behavior used by Fortune 500 companies and small businesses in over 90 countries and 40 different languages.

Marston was interested in using practical explanations to help people understand and manage their experiences and relationships. His research revealed that we communicate in four distinct styles and that while people use all four styles, most have one that is dominant. The best way to establish rapport and trust with someone

39

is to communicate with them using *their* preferred style.

I often use the DISC behavior model in various ways to help my clients and their teams recognize their distinct styles. We then constructively align their communication, leading to improved results.

DISC can help with:

- Hiring and Screening
- Team Building
- Conflict Management
- Leadership Development
- Coaching
- Sales
- Customer Service

"My staffing firm values using the DISC, Motivators & Attributes report for our hires. Having the ability to see a potential employee's motivators really adds another dimension to our interview process. Being aware of someone's motivators allows us to determine if we even have the right environment for them to thrive. Having insights into their unique combination of communication and traits leads to a better understanding of each unique candidate and how well they will collaborate with our team dynamics. It elevates our interview process to a more productive and effective level that everyone appreciates." —Tiffany Stuart, president, Dynamic Office & Accounting Solutions

Not all DISC instruments available in the marketplace are created equal. It is analogous to buying a cup of coffee. There are many different kinds: Starbucks, Peet's, 7-Eleven, and others. All offer coffee; the experience, taste, and cost, however, are vastly different.

Some DISC instruments are basic, unverified, and even free, while others are highly validated and can cost hundreds of dollars. When deciding which DISC tool to use, you should consider the purpose of its use. It's one thing if you are looking to simply gain a little personal insight, and it's quite another when you seek reliable data in order to make key decisions and leverage your and your team's ASSets.

DISC is not a measurement of a person's intelligence, skills, experience, education, or values. DISC is, however, a powerful tool. It is the universal language of human behavior, and how we act is an integral part of who we are. When understood and applied properly, DISC enhances who we are and how we interact in the world.

So, what does "DISC" mean?

DISC is an acronym, with each letter representing one of four styles. Depending on the instrument, the names can be slightly different (e.g., "D" can stand for Dominant, Decisive, Director, etc.).

We each have all four DISC styles present in us, yet the proportions of these styles are unique to each individual. Imagine a recipe with four key healthy ingredients. Change the quantity of any one of the ingredients and the result will be different. As with the ingredients in a recipe, how much "D," "I," "S," and "C" we have in us informs our preferences and behavior.

Each style has its own communication preferences, and those preferences are what largely influence what we want and need from others. When we interact, we have a bias towards our own style, and we often unintentionally judge people harshly whose styles differ from our own.

Do you like things fast or slow? How much information do you prefer to have? Do you need a lot of time to think things through or do you usually make decisions very quickly? Are you energized or exhausted when around high-energy people or situations?

If you prefer fast, does it drive you nuts when people hesitate or seem stuck in analysis paralysis? Or, if you process more slowly and thoughtfully, does it irritate you when others are fast and loud, rushing you or themselves?

More importantly, do you notice the answers to these questions when dealing with other people? The answers are likely to be different from your own! Hence the powerful tool.

There is no right or wrong style; one is not better than another. Each has both great and challenging aspects. Becoming aware of your own preferences provides you the opportunity not only to align with others but to adjust and balance your strengths and manage or minimize your overextensions. Realizing it's not a one-size-fits-all communication world gives you a leg up on better understanding and relating with others and their varying styles.

Though we all are a blend of the styles, let's take a look at the pure styles and consider what each type tends to look for in communication.

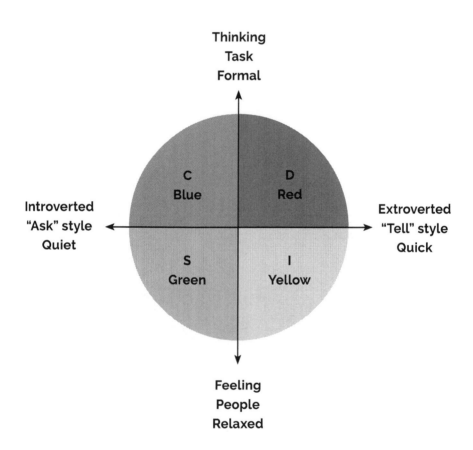

D Style: Director/Dominant/Decisive
The "D" is looking for...RESULTS

- AMBITIOUS, FORCEFUL, DECISIVE
- INDEPENDENT, CHALLENGING
- BOTTOM-LINE ORGANIZER
- SELF-STARTER, FORWARD LOOKING
- VALUES TIME, CHALLENGE ORIENTED
- COMPETITIVE, HIGHLY ACTIVE
- NOT CONTENT WITH STATUS QUO
- INNOVATIVE AND TENACIOUS
- STAND BACK AND LET THIS PERSON GO

I Style: Influencer
The "I" is looking for...The EXPERIENCE

- EXPRESSIVE, ENTHUSIASTIC, FRIENDLY
- DEMONSTRATIVE, TALKATIVE, STIMULATING
- OPTIMISTIC, A CREATIVE PROBLEM-SOLVER
- MOTIVATED TOWARDS GOALS, HUMOROUS
- TEAM PLAYER, GOOD NEGOTIATOR,
- VERBALIZES ARTICULATELY

S Style: Steadiness/Stabilizing
The "S" is looking for...SECURITY

- METHODICAL, SYSTEMATIC, RELIABLE
- STEADY, RELAXED, MODEST
- DEPENDABLE TEAM PLAYER
- A HARD WORKER FOR THE RIGHT LEADER
- A GREAT LISTENER, PATIENT, EMPATHETIC, CALMING AND STABILIZING, LOGICAL
- A STEP-WISE THINKER
- GOOD AT COMPLETING TASKS
- LOYAL

C Style: Compliance/Cautious
The "C" is looking for...INFORMATION
- ANALYTICAL, CONTEMPLATIVE
- CONSERVATIVE, EXACTING
- CAREFUL AND DELIBERATE
- AN OBJECTIVE THINKER, CONSCIENTIOUS, MAINTAINS HIGH STANDARDS
- TASK ORIENTED, DIPLOMATIC
- DETAIL ORIENTED, DEFINE, CLARIFY
- GET INFORMATION, CRITICIZE, TEST
- PAY ATTENTION TO SMALL DETAILS

EXTROVERTED OR INTROVERTED?
HIGH "D" AND HIGH "I" = **EXTROVERTED**
HIGH "S" AND HIGH "C" = **INTROVERTED**

PEOPLE OR TASK ORIENTED?
HIGH "I" AND HIGH "S" = **PEOPLE ORIENTED**
HIGH "D" AND HIGH "C" = **TASK ORIENTED**

There are certain behaviors associated with different styles. For example, "D" and "I" are both extroverted types, whereas the "S" and "C" are introverts. The "D" and "C" are process oriented, while the "I" and "S" are people oriented.

Are you primarily an extrovert or an introvert? How about people or process oriented? Perhaps a close mix of both? Some of us are ambiverts: we are part extrovert and part introvert, having characteristics of each.

When reading the above communication style descriptions, did you notice how different the styles truly are? Can you see why some people just seem to push your buttons? Most often, those who frustrate or confuse us simply have a different communication style. Often we judge people as wrong when they just approach situations from a different perspective.

Are you beginning to see how important it is to recognize and understand our different communication styles? **Shifting from good to great communication involves understanding your own style as well as that of others, and using the information constructively.** Seek to understand and meet people where they are. It doesn't work to try and change someone. In essence, it is better to respect your different perspectives and manage everyone's expectations.

Fundamentally, we all have a need to be heard. To feel accepted. As you understand others more, they will feel understood.

To help you to recognize and treat people the way they want to be treated, see the chart below.

Recognizing DISC Behavior Styles

Color	Style	Introverted or Extroverted	People or Process	Looks for
RED	D - Dominant/ Decisive	Extroverted	Process- Direct	RESULTS
YELLOW	I - Influencer/ Interactive	Extroverted	People- Friendly	THE EXPERIENCE
GREEN	S - Steadiness/ Stabilizing	Introverted	People- Cooperative	SECURITY
BLUE	C - Compliance/ Cautious	Introverted	Process- Analytical	INFORMATION

With so much of our communication being virtual, it's also important to remember that the same principles apply to written communication. Years ago, I was interviewed by the *Wall Street Journal* on the topic of email communication misfires. I emphasized that when writing emails, we need to consider these different communication styles to achieve the best results.

Here is a brief overview of the four styles and considerations to take, specifically when sending email:

D – Dominance. The High D Dominant person is after RESULTS. Provide clear, specific, and brief points. If you need to include details in your email, ensure that the main point is made in the first sentence or two, as there is a good chance that a "High D" will not read your entire email. If you receive a short email that seems abrupt, it may be that the sender is a "High D."

I – Influence. The High I Influencer is after the EXPERIENCE. Set a friendly and fun tone in your email. Don't jump straight into business. They want to feel connected with the writer, acknowledged, and thus appreciate enthusiasm.

S – Steadiness. The High S Steadiness person needs to feel SECURE. They are steady, logical, and undemonstrative. They do not like change, so ensure that any emails help them to understand, are based in logic, and address their need for security. Be sincere and follow through.

C – Compliance. The High C Compliant person is after INFORMATION. They are analytical, risk-averse, and have a high need for data, structure, and order. When communicating with them, give them the data (use charts, graphs, and stats when possible). Also, avoid being overly personal or demanding. Provide them with a reasonable timetable and enough information to make them feel comfortable.

So how exactly do we know what a person's communication style is? Ideally, we use available tools and training to learn our own style and identify the styles of others.

We are not all hardwired the same way. Each of us has our unique "code" that makes us most accessible. Only when you understand each person's communication preferences can you crack the code to achieve great communication with them.

Ultimately, better understanding and communication will help your entire team more effectively work their ASSets off.

"Most people do not listen with the intent to understand. Most people listen with the intent to reply."
—Stephen R. Covey, author of
The 7 Habits of Highly Effective People

truth #5

Truth #5: People Are Hired Because of Their Skills but Fired for Not Being Liked

Lie #5: Being great at what we do is enough.

"The person who gets hired is not necessarily the one who can do that job best but the one who knows the most about how to get hired."
—Richard Nelson Bolles, author of
What Color Is Your Parachute?

WHETHER YOU WORK IN A SMALL BUSINESS or large organization, it's not enough to be great at WHAT you do. Success also depends on HOW you do it and WHO you are doing it with. Specifically, how well you get along with others.

I'm not suggesting that everyone has to love you or invite you over for dinner. However, fostering healthy relationships with your executive team, peers, subordinates, vendors, and clients will serve you well beyond any technical skills and talents you may have.

You may be a rock-star contributor, but if you can't get along with people, your job or business may not be as secure as you think.

This can be a problem for technical leaders in particular. Having great technical abilities does not necessarily translate into effective leadership or good people skills.

When we scan our mental Rolodex of colleagues, we may find that some people genuinely like us, some don't, and many are probably neutral. Bottom line: just how likable are we? A constructive way to go about determining this is to answer the following questions:

1. Do you listen to understand?
2. Are you confident yet not arrogant?
3. Are you receptive to constructive feedback or are you defensive?
4. Do you try to take credit for yourself or easily share credit with others?
5. Do you take responsibility or tend to pass the blame on to others?
6. Do you take into account each person's individual communication style, and do you adjust your own communication style with others? Remember DISC?

Your skills may have landed you your job or started your business, but how well you get along with others may determine whether you excel and keep it!

"Not everyone thinks the way you think, knows the things you know, believes the things you believe, nor acts the way you would act. Remember this and you will go a long way in getting along with people."
—Arthur Forman, English schoolmaster

CASE STUDY

An HR executive of a winery engaged my coaching assistance on behalf of the winery's CFO, whom we'll call Ted. She explained that while Ted was very good at his job and instrumental in helping the winery prepare to go public, he just wasn't a team player. In fact, the executive team was disturbed by Ted's apparent lack of interaction. He normally isolated himself in his office with his door closed and showed no interest or enthusiasm towards them or others.

To them, Ted was a problem they wanted fixed. Little did they realize, though, that they themselves contributed to the problem by judging Ted based on their own unconscious bias. Simply put, they expected Ted to behave more like them.

Except for Ted, the executive team members all happened to be extroverted, highly interactive, and sociable. Ted's quiet demeanor was off-putting to them because it seemed to show a lack of enthusiasm. As a result, they determined he simply was not a good team player.

During my first meeting with Ted, it became obvious to me that he was very committed to the team and their shared goals but that he was an extreme introvert. Ted saw himself as a team player who had been doing important work to position their organization to go public, benefiting everyone. He really wasn't interested in socializing and was instead immersed in his work, which was both highly strategic and detailed.

Ted shared that he is a chess player, so I compared his work and relationships to a chess game, emphasizing that every move was vital for a win.

In discussing the idea of executive coaching, Ted wasn't particularly receptive at first, saying, "I'm an old bird and don't see myself changing who I am at this stage." I reassured him that I had no intention, nor power, to change him. Rather, I could help him identify and leverage his strengths while managing any blind spots and expectations of his peers.

Coaching became another important chess move helping to facilitate his and the organization's success. Fortunately, Ted began to relax and welcome my help. This was good news for Ted and the team, as not everyone is coachable. When we are set in our ways, unaware and uncoachable, we certainly are working much harder than we need to.

First, I had Ted complete a DISC assessment. The results confirmed what I had expected. Highly introverted, he had little need to connect, relate, or be liked. Since he was hardwired to analyze data and produce highly accurate and detailed work, his skills and communication style were perfectly aligned to the job with which he was tasked. His communication style, however, was radically different from that of his peers. Understanding and managing this difference would benefit everyone.

In a relatively short time, Ted became more self-aware, realizing that there was a place for everyone's style, including his. He didn't have to change who he was; rather, he began to make small, manageable changes—and so did his peers. The results were dramatic.

One of the complaints about Ted had been his "hiding out" all the time. In our discovery, I learned that Ted wasn't holding regular meetings with his team members, which made him seem disinterested and inaccessible. Ted agreed that two team meetings a month would be both entirely reasonable and comfortable.

Ted had a small team of eight that he managed, including a direct report, whom we'll call Jeff. Jeff interacted rather well with Ted, along with the rest of their team. We discussed having Ted manage his role similar to a "politician"—utilizing Jeff as his "campaign manager."

Ted could impart his priorities and updates to Jeff, and Jeff would then serve as a spokesperson on behalf of Ted, using "we" language. This way others knew Ted was part of the communication. Ted became more visible both directly and indirectly by having Jeff represent him.

While that progressed, the HR executive realized that she and others had held a biased opinion of Ted, with whom they found it difficult to connect. With a deeper understanding of his natural style, she not only learned to accept and appreciate Ted more, she conveyed this to the rest of the executive team, who also became more understanding.

Together, everyone became better at managing expectations of one another.

Differences in personality types often lead to poor communication. Even when executives are high-level performers, contributing greatly to the success of their organizations, they can be viewed as difficult, overbearing, obnoxious, impulsive, demanding, impatient, disengaged, critical, negative, unenthusiastic, or detached.

Hence, it is key to create an environment that recognizes the value of having a team that is not only diverse in their skills and talents but also in their styles. The very traits that afford our success should not be the same ones that alienate us! The key is to stay true to who we are, aligning ourselves with our roles, while remaining aware that others are often (yes, always) different.

We also have to manage expectations. If everyone on a team achieves this goal, then they will be on their way to working their ASSets off and achieving extraordinary success.

"Ninety percent of the art of living consists of getting along with people you cannot stand."
—Samuel Goldwyn, film producer

truth #6

Truth #6: ShiFt Happens When You Leverage Your Team's Strengths

Lie #6: We have to do everything ourselves.

"None of us is as smart as all of us."
—Ken Blanchard, author of
The One Minute Manager

ARISTOTLE SAID THAT "the whole is greater than the sum of its parts." In other words, when individual parts are connected to form one entity, they are worth more than if the parts were separate.

We already understand the importance of aligning ourselves with our natural talents and interests. The same principle applies to teams.

Understanding, aligning, respecting, and leveraging our individual and collective skills, talents, and communication styles allows us to truly work our ASSets off.

Imagine you're at a baseball game and a fly ball is hit to the outfield. Should your first baseman run to catch the ball? Would it work for two or three players to stand just below the fly ball, gloves in the air—ready—but then not "call it," letting the ball drop right between them? Of course not!

Just like in a winning baseball team, we need to:

1. Cover all the bases.
2. Have players that understand, like, and are capable in their respective roles.
3. Have clear expectations, responsibilities, and accountabilities for each position on the team.
4. Have players call it when they have it.
5. Catch the ball!
6. Congratulate and celebrate the wins. (Note: unlike in sports, don't pat your ASSets.)

Same as in baseball, successful businesses rely on high-performing teams, not on an owner who tries to cover all the bases alone. Great leaders understand that and focus on discovering not only their own natural talents and interests but also those of the group. That leads us to the next important topic: delegation.

Believing that you have to do everything yourself is working hard. If you find yourself doing this, it may be due to your mind-set, circumstances, or both.

Delegating effectively starts with a willingness to involve and trust others. If you resist delegating, it would be helpful to consider the reasons why. Perhaps you have a need for control. Or you lack trust in others. If it is either of these things, it is important to consider why. What are your expectations, and do you have the right team members in the right roles? Delegating doesn't mean dumping or abdicating. Thoughtful delegation keeps in mind each person's skills, natural style, interests, and values. Both the delegator and the person to whom work is being delegated are equally responsible for success.

Great leaders aren't great at everything; they are great at identifying and delegating to the strengths of their team.

So how do we assemble a winning team?

Not everyone is just like you, nor should they be. Surround yourself with your "complements," people who bring perspectives, styles, and strengths that differ from yours. Have them on your team. You can work your ASSets off by cultivating diversity within your organization.

There are many great tools to help you better understand your team's talents. Some of the widely used assessment instruments for organizations include Strength Finders, Myers-Briggs, and the previously touched-on DISC.

My tool of choice is the EEOC-compliant, enhanced DISC: the Innermetrix ADVanced Insights Profile, which combines the best of three world-class profiles.

The Innermetrix ADVanced Insights Profile includes the **Attribute Index,** which measures how one thinks and makes decisions; the **Values Index,** which measures motivational styles and drivers; and the **DISC Index,** which measures preferred behavioral and communication styles.

Together they answer the questions WHAT? WHY? and HOW?

- What natural talents do you have?
- Why are you motivated to use them?
- How do you prefer to use them?

Innermetrix Inc. notes that the ADVanced Insights Profile is unique in that it:

- has the highest validity and reliability scores on the market today
- was the first attribute instrument to measure over seventy business-related competencies
- uses a one-of-a-kind click-and-drag interface for significantly greater accuracy and ease of use
- contains the most current instrument items for increased accuracy and reliability.

In his book *What's Your Genius?*, Jay Niblick, Innermetrix Inc. founder and CEO, shares compelling information regarding human behavior, resulting from a seven-year human performance study known as the Genius Project. The study involved 197,000 individuals across twenty-three countries, using the scientifically validated Innermetrix Attribute Index. "Genius," as defined by Niblick, was descriptive of a person's ability to perform, due to his or her own natural talents.

The study statistically compared the most and least successful people, measuring each individual's ability in a wide variety of attributes relevant to performance. They endeavored to understand the differences between the best and the rest.

They discovered that there is no one "Genius Talent"—no correlation to specific skill sets. Instead, *self-awareness* and *authenticity* were present at higher levels in the best performers. In fact, **when studying effort versus success, there was a 100% correlation to self-awareness and authenticity.**

Rather than seeking to eliminate weaknesses by developing themselves, **geniuses eliminate the weakness by removing their dependence on it.** This analysis required clear understanding by these individuals of "how they worked" in these challenging situations. Understanding yourself is key to achieving peak performance in any role or endeavor.

When applying this awareness to teams, you can better understand, communicate with, motivate, and ultimately leverage your team's strengths. In this study, each successful "genius" also had a person or process to complement them. No one can do it alone! So why try and lead your team from a one-size-fits-all mind-set, or attempt to change people to conform to your expectations? That is working hard.

Working your ASSets off means hiring, managing, motivating, and developing team members while being cognizant of their natural personal styles, talents, and core values. This is optimal organizational alignment.

On the subject of motivating team members, let's turn to a subject matter expert.

New York Times best-selling author Daniel H. Pink has written several books on business, work, and behavior. In his TED Global 2009 talk "The Puzzle of Motivation" (with over 22 million views), Pink shares science and fact on the subject of extrinsic and intrinsic motivation. He shines a light on the fact that the outdated "carrots and sticks" system of rewards and punishment most often doesn't work in our current century. He explains that "too many organizations are making their decisions, their policies, about talent and people, based on assumptions that are outdated, unexamined, and rooted more in folklore than in science." Furthermore, he said, "If we really want high performance, we need a new approach around intrinsic motivation."

Just as the "carrot and stick" rewards-and-punishment system is largely ineffective for most businesses, so is the antiquated employee performance feedback process.

Let's consider how we give and receive feedback. For years, the industry norm for helping employees improve their performance was to use ineffective reviews that were as painful for the reviewer as for the employee. This process has never really worked and has been the subject of much research over the last few decades. The sad thing is, some research suggests that reviews are actually counterproductive. It seems that telling people what we think of their performance and how they should improve not only fails to help but can actually *hinder* learning.

In part, this is true because humans are unreliable evaluators of other humans, as our evaluations are largely influenced by both our own conscious and unconscious biases. Earlier, I shared that we are not all hardwired the same way. Influenced both by genetics and early childhood development, the wiring of our brain is unique. We simply aren't set up to learn the same way. Then, throughout our lives, as our brains continue to develop, the developmental path follows our own particular strengths and proclivities.

In their *Harvard Business Review* (March–April 2019) article "The Feedback Fallacy," Marcus Buckingham and Ashley Goodall point out that "focusing people on their shortcomings doesn't enable learning; it impairs it." That "neurologically, we grow more in our areas of greater ability (our strengths are our development areas)" and that "learning is less a function of adding something that isn't there than it is of recognizing, reinforcing, and refining what already is."

If our brain grows most where it is strongest, trying to focus on improving our shortcomings, whether yours or others, is ineffective at best. Instead, we need to identify, align, and reinforce the skills at which we naturally excel.

CASE STUDY

Working with a small 30-person IT company, we assessed the growing needs of the business as compared to their leadership talent, strengths, and interests.

Together we created an organizational chart based on their vision for the next 3 to 5 years. This helped them crystallize what their needs were. Only then did we turn our attention to which members of the existing team were best aligned with each available role. The chart also revealed what was missing: a de facto gap analysis.

(Tip: A creative, practical, and effective way to do this is to use sticky notes on a large wall. Start with an org chart of the roles needed today and then create another one as if you were operating from your 3- to 5-year vision state. It's important to remember to use roles rather than people as you create your vision. Only after all of the roles are established do you then begin to compare them with team members already on your bench. Then you may identify which people match which roles and what might be lacking. Use your cell phone to take photos of the configurations, which can later be used to formalize the org chart.)

With the IT company, we began by aligning areas of responsibility with each of the three owner-leaders. For each, we matched 5 to 6 key accountabilities. The result was that their previous areas of responsibility (which had been only loosely defined) were tightened into clearly defined roles that aligned with each of their strengths.

As important as these role definitions were, it was equally crucial to discover those areas of responsibility that weren't naturally aligned with any of their talents or interests. We then created an interim plan for who was going to do what in these areas, bringing in non-partners to assist. This way, the organization was able to move forward in a concise and far more productive fashion.

No matter the size or nature of an organization, this can be done. If you don't have a large internal team, you can simply use outside resources to fulfill some of the areas of responsibility. Engage others who have the natural talent and interest in those areas where you and your team members currently need support. Contracting experts via outsourced talent in certain functional disciplines (accounting or marketing, for instance) is often an ongoing strategic solution. Or this can be temporary, as a stopgap measure while you add new team members.

With the right team that is leveraging its strengths, you can all work your ASSets off and reach the long-lasting success you envision.

truth #7

Truth #7: It Is Important to Know What's Working and What's Not

Lie #7: We can assume everything is fine.

"Keep learning; don't be arrogant by assuming that you know it all, that you have a monopoly on the truth; always assume that you can learn from someone else."
—Jack Welch, former chairman and CEO of General Electric

BY NOW, WE REALIZE the value of understanding ourselves and others. Now, let's also check in on understanding our situations.

Can you make an honest assessment of how things are going within your company, department, or team? If you are the leader, how effective are you? Are you sure of that? How can you be?

Without a truly honest understanding of how things are going, we continue to work blind. **If you want to work your ASSets off instead, take inventory of what's working and what's not.**

Taking inventory in business and in life serves as a reality check that we all need regularly. "When you know better, you do better," as wisely stated by writer and poet Maya Angelou.

Oftentimes, we operate on autopilot, much like we do when we drive our cars to familiar places. Ever catch yourself arriving at your destination and not really remembering how you got there? Or perhaps you were unsure as to whether you locked your house, closed your garage door, or turned off the coffeepot?

Our awareness tends to be dulled by routine. We can easily become too comfortable or complacent, thinking everything is great, even when it isn't. Keeping tabs on what matters will help us proactively address issues before they sneak up and overtake us. Stepping back and taking a fresh look through the lens of an *ON perspective* versus an *IN perspective* can produce invaluable insights and opportunities to work better, smarter, easier, and happier.

Here's a case in point. A CEO, whom we'll call Mark, owned a $30 million promotional product business. When asked to describe his leadership style, he responded with "my team loves me," and "everyone respects me." He emphatically believed this to be true. What he didn't realize was that his employees were only telling him what he wanted to hear.

His company had declining profits, his employees were experiencing a high level of stress, turnover was high, and morale was low.

Undertaking a discovery process, I learned that several employees were frustrated working with Mark. They described Mark as controlling and defensive. Rather than run the risk of confrontation or any consequences stemming from bringing up the issues, employees just went along. That is, until they didn't, and quit.

Mark was unaware of the difficulties and focused more on his own workload in an attempt to reach goals for the company. He had a particularly hard time delegating and also didn't seem to understand, align, or motivate his employees. When they quit, he blamed the high turnover on market conditions, such as industry competition and the low unemployment rate.

While it was initially hard for Mark to accept his shortcomings, through thoughtful and supportive coaching feedback, he soon realized that he was out of touch with how disengaged his employees were and how his approach had contributed to their current state. He acknowledged that they were working hard rather than working their ASSets off.

Resolved to turn things around, Mark committed himself and began to shift the company culture by trying to better understand his team and develop himself as a leader. Through executive coaching, peer advisory support, and team talent analysis, Mark became a more strategic CEO and less of a controlling micromanager. One year later, employee morale had improved, retention was up, and the company's profitability had jumped 28%!

Looking at Mark's team, we can see just how unknowingly destructive it is to run a business with disengaged employees. There are plenty of statistics showing that Mark's firm is not an exception. In fact, the state of mind of most workers in the U.S. is pretty dismal. Only 33% of employees in the United States are actually engaged in their work, according to Gallup's "State of the American Workplace" report of February 2017. This means over two-thirds of employees nationwide aren't working their ASSets off in their jobs. Over the past decade, Gallup has surveyed more than 10 million people worldwide on the topic of employee engagement (or how positive and productive people are at work). In his book *Strengths Finder 2.0*, Tom Rath wrote that Gallup's studies "indicate that people who have the opportunity to focus on their strengths every day are six times as likely to be engaged in their jobs and more than three times as likely to report having an excellent quality of life in general."

This is why it pays to work your ASSets off! If you can engage your employees, you can enjoy the benefits of leading a more satisfied and productive team.

After conducting research and having open conversations with employees at Mark's company, I recommended we evaluate the situation from the top down. From his leadership style to how things were working (or not) within the company, we took an honest look at all of the key areas. This provided us with a guide for where to focus attention and resources. Mark's willingness to listen and actually hear and internalize some tough conversations were paramount to the ensuing success story. We can all benefit from regularly asking ourselves and our teams, *What's working and what's not?*

So how do we get started?

There are a lot of assessments and surveys available, such as 360s, or you can use a customized process.

For a business with an executive management team, a good high-level business assessment tool is the Innermetrix Organizational Health Check-Up (OHC). I especially like to use this with management teams in closely held businesses or partnerships. Learning whether the team is on the same page is as relevant as the check-up information itself.

The OHC explores fifty-five essential elements for optimal business performance.

The eleven core business dimensions that drive performance and profitability are:

1. **Personal** – How does the individual feel in the organization?
2. **Employee Alignment** – Is everyone driving results and profitability?
3. **Personnel** – How effectively do your leaders lead?
4. **Team Effectiveness** – How strong are your teams?
5. **Leadership** – How trusted and inspiring is your leadership?
6. **Strategy & Planning** – How secure is your strategy?
7. **Customer Service** – How loyal are your customers?
8. **Sales & Marketing** – Does your pitch resonate and sell?

9. **Operations** – Do you run efficient and quality operations?
10. **Cultural** – How cohesive and beneficial is your culture?
11. **Management** – How effectively do you manage things?

Oftentimes, examining these questions in order to assess key areas that might need attention is enough to effect change. It can reawaken us from a sleepwalking state, giving us the heightened awareness necessary to strategically address any issues.

If it's necessary to dive more deeply, beyond the management team, I find it effective to gather feedback from other team members through an interactive, facilitated *What's Working and What's Not* session.

"Our business coach, Allison, conducted a 'What's Working and Not Working' exercise with our staff. This exercise has helped my partner and me keep a pulse on our staff's job satisfaction, learn what is important to them in their professional lives, and provide a report card on our efforts to provide an ideal work environment. It has allowed us to make small changes that have made a big impact AND it gave the staff a voice that was heard, even if we couldn't make all the changes requested. Our staff expressed sincere appreciation for the opportunity to express themselves!" —Kimberly Johnson, co-owner and managing director, EJA Lighting Design

What's Working and What's Not Session

This kind of session tends to be most useful when led by an unbiased, experienced professional facilitator.

PHASE I

• Team members, excluding managers and owners, are invited to openly and confidentially share in small groups of up to twenty-five their feelings about what is working and what is not.

• The facilitator is responsible for managing constructive feedback, maintaining a safe and respectful environment, and encouraging full participation. The more honest and meaningful the feedback about the team and organization, the more insight we have to work with.

- During the exercise, it is important that the facilitator build trust and rapport with the team members so that they feel safe to openly share. Employees may be concerned about possible consequences or retaliation for any sharing they provide. The feedback gathered should never identify who shared it. Confidentiality is critical for eliciting honest and useful feedback. The initial shares are usually the hardest to get, but once the process gets started, additional participation follows rather easily.

- The facilitator must also manage expectations and constructiveness. Identifying what isn't working is not an invitation for participants to insult, complain, or blame. Also, the participants must understand that sharing their feedback doesn't mean that everything they've identified will necessarily be addressed in the manner they'd like. The owner/executive will ultimately prioritize what, if any, changes will be made.

- No problem solving takes place during this phase. The only purpose of these meetings is to gather the data. Analysis and solution development take place during a later phase.

PHASE II

- All feedback gathered by the facilitator is pooled, prioritized, and summarized into a categorized report for the executive management team. Some examples of What's Working and What's Not categories include:
  - Workflow
  - Environment
  - Leadership
  - Communication
  - Company Culture
  - HR/Benefits
  - Finance
  - Communication
  - Sales & Marketing

- Relaying the feedback to the management team also requires experienced guidance. Some leaders can be hard on themselves, taking feedback personally. For the process to be constructive, it is important that they receive and process feedback through a receptive and objective lens, respecting the anonymity of the participants' individual comments.

• From the captured feedback, the management team prioritizes any necessary changes. The list may be short or long, so they have to manage their own expectations, as well as those of others. It is unrealistic to try and address or solve everything at once, so focusing on one to three items with the highest potential impact is a good place to start.

PHASE III

• Once the management team prioritizes which items they want to address, the full team, including the managers, gathers together.

• The initial team is thanked for their contributions in identifying What's Working and What's Not.

• The identified priority items are shared with everyone.

• Together, the team constructively offers possible suggestions and solutions to any items identified for focused improvement. Management and ownership maintain a collaborative, objective, respectful process to benefit all. Management is encouraged to not come with ready-made solutions that may stifle the creative sharing of ideas. Also, they are directed to refrain from cutting people off or shooting ideas down. As with the process of gathering the data, you want all ideas to be fully and respectfully expressed. The opportunity to further evaluate ideas can follow.

WE ARE REMINDED BY MOTIVATIONAL SPEAKER SIMON SINEK that "the role of a leader is not to come up with all the great ideas. The role of a leader is to create an environment in which great ideas can happen."

The importance of taking inventory of what's working and what's not working holds true not only in business but also in life. Checking in with yourself, assessing what, if any, changes you may want to make, is key for personal success. This especially holds true for leaders, as it is common for leaders to discover that what's not working in their personal lives mirrors similar failings in their businesses.

Personal Inventory

Below is a Personal Inventory checklist offering some key areas you may want to reflect on during your self-assessment.

Before jumping in, let's manage our expectations. Taking inventory is not an invitation to beat yourself up for not meeting an impossible standard.

Thinking that we can live perfectly balanced lives is delusional. Even believing there is such a thing as a perfectly balanced life may cause you to chase the improbable, if not impossible, and will likely lead to frustration and disappointment. The reality is that our attention and effectiveness may shift from one area to another, depending on our current circumstances, priorities, and focus. We are living a **blended life** and at any time, we can intentionally shift the composition of our blend.

Rather than try to measure up to a standard of perfect balance, instead consider what really matters to you and what you would like to change in your blend.

Even if every area matters equally, pick just one or two to focus on at once. When you reach the desired state of improvement that you are able to maintain for at least three weeks, you can shift your attention to another area.

One way to easily "find" balance is to proactively engage in compound experiences. You can do this by incorporating multiple areas of importance or interest into the same activities. I call them "2-fers," where you are able to tend to two areas of interest at the same time. For example, much of my work time is spent indoors with clients in conference rooms or offices. So, for me, getting enough outdoor time can be challenging. One way I manage to squeeze more of the outdoors into my life is by driving my convertible. I have to get from point A to point B regardless, so I might as well enjoy the sun and open air while on my way.

A favorite weekly ritual of mine is actually a "3-fer." For years, in addition to regularly hitting the gym, I've also walked around a beautiful reservoir every weekend. I schedule the walk with various friends and colleagues so that I can get some quality time catching up while also exercising outdoors. My two-loop (six-mile) weekly ritual feeds multiple needs at the same time: exercising, being outdoors, and spending time with friends.

For me, anything that's not on my calendar is just a wish. Anything that is important to me is on my calendar. I choose not to leave my exercise, outdoor time, or friendship hours to chance or as a to-do-list checkbox. My personal priorities, not just my business activities, are on my calendar. While writing this book, I created a new ritual with protected, scheduled time for writing. At times, for my 2-fer, I reviewed and edited my work while pedaling a stationary bike at the gym or while sitting in my backyard. The key is to find compatible, not competing, activities. For example, taking paperwork out on a date night may be multitasking, but it doesn't qualify as a constructive 2-fer.

Think about your priorities and your own calendar. How committed are you to what you say matters? Is it scheduled on your calendar? Do you have as much integrity with an appointment with yourself as with a client? Use the personal inventory list below to assess and identify areas where you may want to pay more attention.

Personal Inventory Checklist

      1. Mind-set

      2. Communication

      3. Relationships (with friends, family, and colleagues)

      4. Rest

      5. Exercise

      6. Being outdoors

      7. Recreation/fun/creativity

      8. Sexual health

      9. Mindfulness

      10. Gratitude practice

      11. Energy

      12. Nutrition

13. Time management/prioritizing

14. Organization

15. Self-care

16. Getting results

17. Connection with community

18. Spirituality

19. Finances

20. Health visits

21. Volunteering

22. Travel

As you think about these areas, consider how you could schedule in more of what is important. Don't forget opportunities for 2-fers or 3-fers! We all have the same 24 hours in a day, 7 days in a week. How you design your "custom blend" can significantly expand the depth of value you get from your time.

truth #8

Truth #8: HOW Is Easy When You Know Your WHY

Lie #8: Knowing how to do things is most important.

> *"Achievement happens when we pursue and attain what we want. Success comes when we are in clear pursuit of why we want it."*
>
> —Simon Sinek, author and motivational speaker

LET'S TALK NOW about what we do and the importance of spending as much time throughout our days on the WHYs as we do on the HOWs. How we spend our days is ultimately how we spend our lives. Are you spending it doing what matters most?

How we do things is a learned behavior. We can acquire knowledge, develop skills, plan, and execute goals successfully. These successes can offer rewards and even pleasure. Meeting goals can be gratifying. Yet the HOW is primarily focused on external action.

So, what does it mean to live from our WHY? This is more internal in nature. Having intrinsic motivation can offer true fulfillment.

Let's consider the difference between **gratification** and **fulfillment.** According to dictionary.com, *gratify* means "to give pleasure to a person (or persons) by satisfying desires or humoring inclinations or feelings," whereas *fulfill* means "to develop the full potential of." As I consider the two words, **gratification** insinuates a temporary external state, whereas **fulfillment** implies a long-lasting internal state.

Understanding what fulfills you and living your life authentically and intentionally will align you with your WHY.

Millions of people have sought their purpose for decades. Many have done so with a great deal of angst, feeling rudderless in a modern and complicated world. Even those considered to be very successful may still find themselves searching. This is usually because there is the relentless feeling that something is missing. They do not feel fulfilled. The short answer to the question "What's my purpose?" is simple but not easy. **Your purpose is to live a fulfilled life.**

What this life looks like is different for everyone. Not everyone will walk on the moon or develop the cure for cancer. Yet we all can make a difference in the world by leading a fulfilling life and helping others around us to do the same.

So how do you find your WHY? Well, it isn't available for purchase, it isn't determined by someone else, and it doesn't come in the form of a checkbox on your to-do list. Understanding your WHY is a discovery process.

Earlier, I shared a few tools and resources that can help you to better understand yourself. The DISC assessment addresses our HOW, and the Values/Motivators section addresses our WHY.

The Values assessment identifies our motivators, ranked in importance.

- **Aesthetic** – Harmony, connection, peace
- **Economic** – Competitive, driven & return on investment
- **Individualistic** – Unique, own way
- **Political** – Driven to lead and take responsibility
- **Altruist** – Driven to help, make a difference
- **Regulatory** – Rules are rules, life is a very specific way
- **Theoretical** – Live to learn

Another way you may explore and discover your WHY is by reading Simon Sinek's books *Start with Why* and *Find Your Why*.

As Richard Bolles did in *What Color Is Your Parachute?*, Sinek's discovery process involves using our stories as a means of bringing to light who we are when we are at our natural best.

In his TED talk with over 44 million views, Sinek introduces the importance of "Why?" as a powerful model for leadership. Using his "golden circle" and the company Apple as an example, he drives home the importance for all businesses to know their WHY.

In the talk, Sinek says, "People don't buy what you do; they buy why you do it. And what you do simply proves what you believe." He goes on to say that "achievement happens when we pursue and attain what we want. Success comes when we are in clear pursuit of why we want it."

Understanding our WHY not only helps us as individuals, it is also a huge boost to business owners, organizations, and their team members.

People who believe in what they do, instead of just working for a paycheck, will put more into their work. When we understand, work, and live from our WHY, both individually and collectively, we are at our best. We are living fulfilled lives and working our ASSets off.

truth #9

Truth #9: Your Network Is One of Your Most Valuable ASSets

Lie #9: Networking is a waste of time.

"Nobody makes it alone. Nobody has made it alone.
And we are all mentors to people
even when we don't know it."
—Oprah Winfrey

NOW THAT WE'VE SPENT SOME TIME discussing how to cultivate our own talents as well as those of our employees and coworkers, let's look at how to cultivate and leverage our larger network.

People who pay more attention to **who is in their network** worry less about how they are going to get where they want to go. Their network helps facilitate their getting to their WHY with much greater ease.

The importance of a healthy network may be obvious, yet not everyone effectively manages or utilizes theirs. Since I consider my network community to be one of my most valuable ASSets, I continuously build, nurture, and leverage it.

If you are committed to working your ASSets off, your network is important. So how would you rate the strength and utilization of your network? Perhaps you recognize an opportunity to work your network more? If not, good for you! But even if you feel you are strong in this area, I hope you discover a few nuggets that will help you to work your network even more effectively.

Like it or not, we all have to network, and entrepreneurs especially have to hone this skill. Now I'm not talking about attending random events, engaging in boring small talk, thoughtlessly exchanging business cards, or just having a large database of contacts.

What really matters is building and maintaining great relationships with other people.

I'm grateful to have discovered the value of relationships very early on in my career. I consider my relationships with others the most influential factor in my success.

Traditional networking simply provides opportunities to meet people and begin to make connections. What matters is everything you do from there to develop, foster, and maintain strong relationships.

My colleague Joe Cristiano, founder and CEO of the Northern California Mentoring Group, credits relationship networking for his rapid career advancement, revenue increases, and profit growth in the multiple companies he's mentored. He said, "I realized that relationship networking was the real big-picture secret sauce."

Establishing a connection with people should be the primary goal when engaging in traditional networking. So often, I see people try to jump from meeting to selling. This is a misguided and ineffective approach to networking and doesn't lead to building the invaluable network of relationships we all need.

Instead of thinking of what people can do for you, it's better to be sincerely interested in others, begin to earn their attention, and establish rapport. That's when the magic happens.

Ready to put this into practice? Networking opportunities await you!

You may be thinking, "Wait, what about doing the things I am naturally talented at? Didn't you just say we should play into our strengths? I'm really not a very good networker, so…?" Yes, it is true that some people are naturally better at networking than others; however, even introverts can work their networking ASSets off. The key is to leverage your unique talents and style to make networking effective for you.

Here are some strategies:

Get out there, and there is everywhere! No matter where you are and what you are doing, so long as you interact with another person, it is a networking opportunity. Treat it as such and you'll be more effective in building your network. I have countless stories, my own and others', of great connections made, many of which have led to opportunities, in the least expected places.

Design your Where. Everyone matters, and it is true that you can find opportunity anywhere. That being said, there is exponential value in determining who matters most, then intentionally placing yourself in the right places with the right people. There is a distinction between general versus strategic networking. To promote having strategic relationships, start with identifying your ideal audience and the environment where you'd likely interact with that audience. Figure out which sandbox they are playing in, and then get playing in the sand.

Your ideal audience may not be the same as the end users of your goods or services. It may instead be with your *power partners*.

I'll share practical examples. In my engineering business, my power partners were primarily architects (commercial and residential), developers, and contractors. We identified where these professionals spent the most time and then placed ourselves there.

The first places were the various trade organizations where architects, developers, and contractors were members, such as the Building Industry Association, American Institute of Architects, International Council of Shopping Centers, the Association of General Contractors, and others. Not only were we members, but we also became actively involved in key organizations. Initially, involvement was through sponsorships and committee positions, and then we moved into strategic leadership roles. Some of my personal roles included being president of two such organizations over the years: the Professional Women in Building of both the Home Building Association (HBA) and the California Building Industry Association (CBIA). Additionally, as a board member of HomeAid, I worked closely with developers and architects to provide temporary housing to the homeless. Where we weren't in leadership roles, we increased visibility through sponsoring and attending targeted events.

Many of these professionals were influencers, not necessarily prospective clients. We didn't have to solicit many projects. Rather, we built strategic relationships that resulted in being invited to participate on projects.

For best results, identify which strategically aligned groups, what frequency, number of events, etc., you will commit to, and then be accountable.

Currently, my most strategic sandbox is a professional group called ProVisors, who serve their clients as trusted advisors. This is a group of high-caliber, experienced professionals including attorneys, accountants, financial advisors, bankers, M&A advisors, and other consultants. It provides me with a bench of experts, many of whom I consider my trusted colleagues. They are available to help my clients, as I am available to help with theirs. Initially a member, I currently serve as group leader for a Bay Area chapter with 30-plus professionals. Many of these professionals have become my power partners and advocates.

Make a great first impression. You only have one chance to make the best first impression you can muster. It only takes between 3 and 7 seconds to make an impression, so why not make it a great one?

- **Be approachable.** Lighten up and have an inviting smile. Smiling "is such a simple, basic rule, yet so many people just don't think about it," says Peter Handal, chairman, CEO, and president of Dale Carnegie & Associates. Dale Carnegie was a pioneer on the subject of networking who in 1936 wrote the iconic and timeless book on networking, *How to Win Friends and Influence People.*

- **Be present and engaged.** Are you scanning the room while you are talking with someone? Are you looking down at your smartphone? Maybe you are thinking about your grocery list or work to-dos? I call this all-too-common occurrence *absence of presence.* People can feel it when you are standing right in front of them and yet are not fully present. So get present; just decide and do it. You'll be amazed at how having a simple awareness of the other person can shift each connection you make to a deeper level.

Communicate with style. Meaning, communicate with the person's style in mind. In Chapter 4, we covered how everyone wants to be treated the way THEY want. Pay attention to the cues they give you. Are they talking fast or slow, loud or soft, being animated or reserved, sharing details or being short? Are they standing close or keeping a distance? All of these observable behaviors are important clues to understanding someone's communication style. Pay attention and respond naturally to their preferences. You'll notice a difference in how they relate to you.

Ease into group conversations. Listen first, and then ease your way into conversations. You can do this by asking a relevant question or offering a related comment. Don't interrupt or try to shift attention to yourself.

Listen to understand, and be curious. Most people listen to respond and love to talk about themselves. This is ineffective, as universally, we all want to be understood. This is why being a sincere and interested listener is so important. Introverts can actually have an advantage here.

Through their active listening, the other person may feel like they had a great conversation, even though the introvert didn't say much. When it comes to pacing, try and strike a healthy balance between speed-dating pace among dozens versus talking with one person the entire time.

Be interesting. Being interesting doesn't mean monopolizing the conversation with all of your fascinating stories. Rather, be prepared to briefly and enthusiastically share information not just about your business but also about your hobbies, unique interests, or distinctions.

Be authentic. Don't try too hard. Just relax and be your natural self. People sense when you are genuine, and it builds trust. Introverts may be surprised to learn that they would do better by just being themselves rather than by trying to act outgoing like some of their peers.

Project confidence. Maybe you naturally have or project confidence. Or perhaps you have to "fake it until you make it." Regardless of the degree of confidence you may actually feel, refrain from overly apologizing or making self-deprecating comments. This is a turn-off and diminishes your credibility.

Be approachable. We become approachable when others discover that we have things in common. Explore and share what you have in common with others. Having shared interests can help make it easier to connect with others. Asking questions is such a great way to find out where common ground may lie.

Offer praise. Giving people your full attention is more than what most people do. Also, you can provide acknowledgment and encouragement when appropriate. Sometimes, we can be stingy with our compliments, so try giving them more freely. If you are thinking something positive to yourself, say it aloud. Receiving sincere praise feels good and can make the person feel more connected to you.

Invite and accept help. People want to help, so allow them the opportunity. It can be a gift for them as much as it is for you. Ideally, it is better to ask for help only after you have given or offered others help, but it isn't always necessary. For example, let's say while you are writing a book you happen to meet a best-selling author. You can mention that as a first-time author, you welcome hearing any lessons they may have learned as an experienced author. Ask whether they'd be willing to schedule a time to share their experience with you. Most people are generous and love to share their knowledge or expertise. Timing and approach can certainly influence their receptivity.

Buddy up. Inviting a colleague to join you at an event can make it easy, fun, and effective. Introduce each other to people you know. If there is a genuine opportunity to say something complimentary about the other person, it is more impactful to do so, rather than "tooting your own horn."

Especially if you are an introvert, having a buddy is a great approach. It is also helpful to network with people you already know, engaging in smaller settings or two-on-one situations. For larger gatherings, consider bringing along another person, as this will make your networking much easier. You can introduce and highlight each other and support one another as needed.

Give generously. Listen for opportunities to assist others. Share information, a resource, or an introduction that would be helpful to someone. Do so without being asked or having any strings attached, as it's not about reciprocity. The people to whom I give are not necessarily the same people who may give generously to me. It's about having a mind-set of generosity and support.

Be prepared. Being prepared is more than just showing up with your business cards.

Set your intention. What is your intention? Is there someone in particular you want to meet? An impression you hope to make? Being aware and having an intentional purpose will help you experience better results.

Prepare your elevator speech. Always be prepared to answer the question, "So, what do you do?" I'm amazed at how often this basic and most frequently asked question leaves many stumbling for an answer. If you can't succinctly describe what you do in an interesting way, you'll miss the opportunity to make the best impression. Practice your 30-second elevator speech so that you can confidently and enthusiastically generate initial understanding and interest. It's like a first date: who wants to hear their date vomit their life history out all at once? Take baby steps.

When someone asks about what you do, they are not interested in a blow-by-blow description of how you do things. Nor are they interested in your running through your entire list of service offerings.

As an example, when asked, I share that I'm a trusted business advisor who works with business owners, executives, and their teams who want to get further faster. I may add that as a professional coach and consultant, I help them with their best thinking, communicating, and doing. Only when I've earned someone's additional interest do I share more, such as that I facilitate communication retreats and workshops, create business plans, and develop leaders through coaching and facilitating CEO peer groups.

If asked how I do that, I may then share even more details, including some methodologies, such as designing custom processes or using assessments and tools such as an Organizational Health Check-Up, the One Page Business Plan, DISC, etc.

Follow up. So, you made some connections. Great. It mustn't end there though! Don't just add more to a stack of business cards you may have rubber-banded together on your desk. Whether you use a manual process or a CRM (customer relationship management) program, have a system in place and follow it diligently. Whenever I get a business card, I write on it where I met the person, the date, and anything memorable or relevant. I invite them to connect through LinkedIn, always sending a personalized request. The next step after that varies. I may send a handwritten note, make an introduction or request, schedule a call, or invite them to get together for coffee.

Brush yourself off. Not everyone will be interested, helpful, or even nice. Don't take it personally. If you are rejected, regroup and move on. You have a tribe to build, and not everyone is interested or even a good fit to belong to it. Be open and receptive and mix it with good judgment and discernment.

truth #10

Truth #10: You Create Your Own Results

Lie #10: Good things come to those who wait.

"Success is a science; if you have the conditions, you get the result."
—Oscar Wilde

"You get in life what you have the courage to ask for."
—Oprah Winfrey

"Nothing will work unless you do."
—Maya Angelou

EVER NOTICED HOW SOME PEOPLE talk about what they want but can't seem to make it happen, yet others seem to achieve remarkable results effortlessly?

Why is this?

Personally, I've always been results-driven. You might say it's in my DNA. For this reason, I think I am particularly attuned to when and why people are successful in achieving their goals. In this chapter, I will share my insights and practical strategies to help you not only wish for remarkable results but actually achieve them. I've framed these strategies in a business context because I am passionate about helping business leaders get further faster. But you can apply the same principles to your personal life and enjoy similar success.

When I co-owned my structural engineering business, I knew that my husband and I were responsible not only for our own results but also for those of our team members. I noticed that not everyone had the same orientation towards results, and even if they did, it wouldn't guarantee success in achieving goals.

This was evident not just in our own business. For almost ten years, I was a member of a peer advisory group that included CEOs of multimillion-dollar companies. Some of my colleagues struggled to get results, while others seemed to easily and effectively accomplish great things. Let's break down why this is the case.

Jack Canfield, originator of the *Chicken Soup for the Soul* inspirational book series, said, "I believe that people make their own luck by great preparation and good strategy." Taking these thoughts further, I believe remarkable results come from simultaneously thinking, planning, and acting strategically. In other words, working your ASSets off.

Too many business owners fall into the trap of working only *IN* and not *ON* their business. Author Michael Gerber addressed this dilemma in his best-selling book *The E-Myth Revisited.* He wrote, "Once you recognize that the purpose of your life is not to serve your business, but that the primary purpose of your business is to serve your life, you can then go to work *on* your business, rather than *in* it, with a full understanding of why it is absolutely necessary for you to do so."

So how do you work *ON* your business? Begin by creating the opportunity for regular strategizing. Step out of day-to-day activities and examine your business from a macro perspective.

Here are a few questions to help you get started in thinking strategically:

- What are you doing? and Where are you heading?
- With whom are you doing it?
- What are you trying to create? and How big or small?
- Where are you doing it?
- Who are your customers?
- What are your customers like?
- Where do your customers hang out?
- What is your culture like?
- What are your core values? What matters?
- What motivates you? and What do you want to get out of it?
- What talent and/or resources do you have versus what you need?

Strategic thinking should be done informally *and* formally, alone *and* with others.

Ever notice that some of your best ideas come when you are showering, taking a bath, driving, or exercising? Creative thinking isn't available on demand, like a movie. So, if you decide "I'm going to be strategic for the next hour," don't expect great ideas to rush to your mind. First, give yourself permission to have unstructured free-thinking time and let your thoughts wander. Change the scenery; go for a walk or participate in creative activities. When you allow your mind to relax and dream, ideas start to develop. I've never heard anyone say, "I had a brilliant idea come to me while I was sitting at my desk."

In addition to free-flowing creative thinking, you'll want to include some structured time for strategic thinking. For this, it is important to engage your peers and stakeholders—going at it alone is working hard.

Brainstorming with other entrepreneurs, successful colleagues, and trusted advisors can help to bring out some of your best thinking.

During the last ten years of leading our structural engineering company, I not only participated in a peer advisory group, I also regularly engaged with other business owners and consultants. Even as a strong and independent person, I recognized the value of collaborating with other leaders. In doing so, I drew support (and energy) from various sources to keep me aware, committed, disciplined, and accountable. In short, collaboration helped me to work my ASSets off. Look around at what opportunities you might have. What professional organizations are available? How can you get involved? Do you know other successful entrepreneurs from whom you can get support and feedback?

Now that we have looked at how to cultivate great ideas, let's move on to how we can translate them into a plan. Proper planning is critical in moving from working *IN* your business to working *ON* your business.

There are many planning tools out there. Personally, I am not a fan of some traditional planning techniques where great brainstorming sessions give birth to binders full of pages that ultimately sit on a bookshelf collecting dust.

Some of my colleagues have had success using the simple and practical One-Page Strategic Plan framework outlined in the book *Mastering the Rockefeller Habits* by Verne Harnish. In the book, Harnish writes, "If you want to teach people a new way of thinking, don't bother trying to teach them. Instead, give them a tool, the use of which will lead to new ways of thinking."

In my engineering business, I used another highly effective tool that helped me achieve my desired results. That tool, which I continue to use today, both for my own business and in helping other business leaders, is the One Page Business Plan created by Jim Horan, president and CEO of the One Page Business Plan Company and author of *The One Page Business Plan.*

The One Page Business Plan WORKS!

Here's what a few clients have to say about it:

"Not only has the One Page Business Plan benefited our organization, it has also contributed substantially to my growth as a business leader. The fact that this is an ongoing, iterative process and not a one-shot task means that we have the opportunity and responsibility to review our objectives, strategies, and action plans on an ongoing basis. We can now depend on having accurate business metrics and laser-focused goals, all of which lead to better overall outcomes. The long-term benefits are tangible." —Jeremy Kushner, CEO, BACS Consulting Group

"I've done business planning before, but usually I make up a plan and then forget it by February. The one-page plan forced me to identify goals and put them all on a single page to which I could refer easily. I keep mine on my desk, where I can see it routinely. Allison helped me to actually quantify those goals. That is the magic of the one page. I don't think the plan would have worked for me without guidance on measuring the efficacy of the plan. The result? I increased new sales by over 50% in a year's time. I got so busy I had to stop and do a second plan on how to grow the business to support my new business. I had help on that one too. Oddly, I didn't have to meet any new people. I just had to remember to connect with my centers of influence on a regular basis. The real pain was getting organized to do the plan. But I far prefer the pain of organizing to the pain of wondering how to increase revenue." —Brian K. Trouette, owner, Trouette Insurance Agency, LLC

Whether using the simple-to-follow do-it-yourself One Page Business Plan workbook or the robust interactive cloud-based plan builder and performance management solution, assisted by a trained certified consultant, the One Page Business Plan helps you focus both on the big picture and the important details. It is a great clarity-building tool to make your thoughts more succinct and to avoid wasting time on less important things.

"Is it time for clearer thinking, better decisions, and more reliable execution?" Jim Horan asks.

The plan uses five very simple questions to capture some of your **best thinking and planning** and convey them on one page. This still leaves the **best acting** (doing) part, but we will come back to that.

Five Key Questions asked by the One Page Business Plan:
1. What are you building? (***Vision***)
2. Why does this business exist? (***Mission***)
3. What business results will you measure? (***Objectives***)
4. How will you build this business? (***Strategies***)
5. What is the work to be done? (***Action Plans***)

Answering the Five Key Questions helps you escape day-to-day reactionary mode and puts you into a more *proactive thinking* mind-set. *Proactive planning* then is nothing but the result of your effectively capturing your ideas and committing to them.

Another critical piece of planning is *tracking:* have quantifiable, measurable results and regularly monitor them.

Consider what is important to track. Then track it!

Imagine yourself vacationing on a tropical island; perhaps you are lounging in a comfortable beach chair, sipping a cocktail. You can't really check in on the business while you are away, nor would you want to. To stay in the loop, however, you can receive a one-way communication (e.g., a text) letting you know the status of key performance indicators. What would those indicators be for YOUR business?

What needs to be measured is unique to each business. For example, if you have a manufacturing company, perhaps your data would include Sales, COGS (Cost of Goods Sold), Inventory, or Shipments. If you have a real estate brokerage, perhaps you would track Gross Commission Income, the number of transactions, dollar value currently in escrow, or how many appointments are set up upon your return. If you are a professional services company, perhaps you would measure cash in the bank, net effective multiplier, work backlog value, DSO (number of days out on accounts receivable), or available lines of credit. This critical information is what helps you to create strong growth objectives.

So just what constitutes a strong objective? Here are some examples of weak versus strong objectives.

Weak:

1. I'm going to grow my business this year.
2. We'll land new clients.
3. We'll expand into new territories.
4. We'll hire more employees.

Strong:

1. Our sales will grow this year from $3 million to $5 million while maintaining profitability at 28%.
2. In addition to retaining 95% of our existing clients, we will add ten new clients with a minimum spend of $100K each.
3. We will expand our territory to include three new western states (Oregon, Nevada, and Washington).
4. We'll hire eight more employees (three area sales managers and five salespeople).

Just as important as what you want to include in your plan is what *not* to include. What do you need to stop doing in order to make room for the things that will help you achieve results? You may need to say no to distractions that hinder achieving your desired results.

With your plan in place, we come to the most crucial piece—action.

Great ideas and plans alone do not translate into great results. You must follow this work with great behaviors.

What does it mean, and just how do we regularly engage in "great behaviors"? Our thinking and planning have helped us create specific and measurable objectives. Now we must mindfully take actions that are aligned with these objectives. For that we need **commitment and discipline.**

We may want certain things, but those wants may not necessarily be reflected in our actions. Just how committed are we to what we say we want? And if we are committed, how disciplined are we to follow through? For some, discipline is intrinsic, while for others it's extrinsic. Know this about yourself. What support might you need to get and stay on track?

Consider the health and fitness industry for an analogy. Fitness clubs make a fortune selling memberships to well-intentioned people, many of whom infrequently or virtually never work out. Why is this? It's not because people like to throw their money away. It's because even people who truly want to lose weight or get healthy often only take the first step of joining a gym but then go no further. They are lacking adequate commitment and/or discipline.

Then, of course, there are the members who do show up regularly and are successful. Some train themselves, others participate in group classes or engage a personal trainer. Some people are self-disciplined, while others need more structure, support, and guidance to get through the process.

All of these methods are fine. The important thing is to recognize what you personally need to be successful and go get it. You may find that your level of commitment and discipline varies in different areas of your life. The key is to make honest assessments of those areas where you have goals and then examine what support you need to have in place to help you meet those goals.

People often don't achieve the results they desire because they fail to effectively link their best thinking to their best planning, or their best planning to their best doing (behaving). Exponential results happen when all three elements—strategic thinking, planning, and doing—are interconnected.

So how are *you* doing with what matters? Step back and take an honest assessment. Ask yourself the following questions:

Thinking

- Do I regularly step back to think and strategize rather than just act or react?
- Do I foster creative thinking?
- Am I clear as to what I want?
- Am I thinking big enough?

Planning

- Do I know what success looks like and how to measure it?
- Do I know what I need to get there?
- Do I have specific goals and timelines?
- Do I have well-developed strategies to achieve my goals?
- Do I know what kind of support I may need?
- Have I identified key people who could help?

Doing

- Do I work *ON* as well as *IN* my business?
- How committed am I to what I want?
- Are my actions reflective of my commitment?
- Do I understand what motivates me?
- Do I hold myself accountable or would I benefit from having an accountability partner?
- Am I engaging my peers and consultants for help?
- Do I acknowledge and celebrate my results?

Whatever your answers are, my hope is that you benefit from honest introspection and can now shift from wanting your desired results to actualizing them. If you commit to making good plans and following through with the right support and accountability, you are on track towards working your ASSets off.

"Words should be used as a tool of communication and not as a substitute for action."
—Anonymous

truth #11

Truth #11: Gratitude Is the Gateway to Happiness

Lie #11: You have to work hard in order to be happy.

"Gratitude is the healthiest of all human emotions. The more you express gratitude for what you have, the more likely you will have even more to express gratitude for."
—Zig Ziglar, author, salesman,
and motivational speaker

DO YOU GIVE YOURSELF PERMISSION to be happy? Have you been conditioned to believe that you are not entitled to experience joy unless you work hard to earn it? Do you feel guilty when you experience joy without having worked super hard for it?

While different in our experiences, styles, values, motivators, and networks, we all have equal and immediate access to one very important ASSet: gratitude.

Gratitude is the universal currency for "buying" a life of happiness.

Many people work harder and harder in search of something better, more, or different. They think happiness is the result of their achievements or the things they have accumulated. Rather, gratitude is a way to appreciate what we have now, instead of always reaching for something new in the hopes it will make us happier.

Grateful people are happier, healthier, more engaged, and more productive.

Neuroscience shows that gratitude literally rewires our brains. There is research which supports that just by acting grateful, we can become grateful.

Not only does gratitude create a more positive and happier emotional state, it actually changes our brains!

According to UCLA's Mindfulness Awareness Research Center, regularly expressing gratitude literally changes the molecular structure of the brain, keeps the gray matter functioning, and makes us healthier and happier.

The impact of living a grateful life is profound in every area of business and life.

I considered myself a fairly grateful person for most of my life. But only when I met best-selling author MJ Ryan, one of the world's authorities on the subject of gratitude, did I begin to understand the full depth of what a heart and mind filled with gratitude does. MJ Ryan's many books include *Attitudes of Gratitude: How to Give and Receive Joy Every Day of Your Life.* She has interviewed people all over the world on the subject of gratitude. MJ shared with me that so many people discover true gratitude only after they experience a significant life event, often a mortality scare. The hope of her work is to help people experience gratitude without having to face trauma.

Her words were a wake-up call for me and radically changed my outlook and actions. I began to incorporate a daily gratitude ritual, acknowledging at least ten things daily for which I am grateful. What I have learned is that **gratitude changes your state of being.** No matter what comes your way, your state of mind and being are the filters through which you experience everything.

I'm no Pollyanna and by no means is my life always perfect. However, focusing on gratitude not only helps me become more present and lifts my spirits, but it also shifts my state to one that attracts more great things. If you elevate your positive and grateful mind-set while magnifying your strengths, you will work your ASSets off with ease and joy.

Tips for getting into a grateful state:
- Identify something you appreciate about someone and tell them
- Pause, notice, and appreciate something in your environment
- Think of something you like/appreciate about yourself
- Keep a gratitude journal
- Use apps (e.g., Headspace, Track Your Happiness, Happify, My Gratitude Journal)
- Say thank you
- Send a thank-you card
- Smile
- Meditate
- Visualize positive circumstances
- Positive affirmations
- Have reminders
- Choose your words wisely

Our brain can be fed with how we want it to think. How we think affects how we feel. Start thinking a grateful life to live a grateful life!

truth #12

Truth #12: Get Your ASSets to Work, and You'll Live Your Best Life!

"People can be really smart or have skills that are directly applicable, but if they don't really believe in it, then they are not going to really work hard."
—Mark Zuckerberg

"Work hard and smart, live passionately and gratefully, leverage your talents and those of others. In doing so, you will work your ASSets off and live your best life."
—Allison Tabor

YOU HAVE AN OPPORTUNITY to build your life around your passion. Developing an understanding of yourself and incorporating your natural talents, skills, and strengths will prepare you to take the right action at the right time to get to your passion.

Easier said than done, right? Sadly, we don't have a crystal ball that points out the way to each right action. So, what then do we do?

The right direction isn't always obvious, yet when we look back, we can see how one circumstance, opportunity, decision, or action led to another. In retrospect, it all makes perfect sense, doesn't it?

Life will unfold for us, yet we can steer our way and correct our course at any time. For many, their way is determined by circumstances that force change upon them. Others recognize subtle clues as to what adjustments are necessary, and they make intentional changes. How comfortable each of us is with embracing change often plays a big part in whether we accept our circumstances as our reality or just the catalyst for making our own new reality.

It is never too late to take charge of your destiny, live your best life, and work your ASSets off. The sooner, the better! Below is a summary of the things you can do to start living your best life right now.

Work Your ASSets Off Tips:

Know yourself. Curiously and honestly explore your communication style, interests, strengths, values, motivators, and challenge areas. Remember that we all have blind spots, so consider feedback from others in addition to your self-assessment.

Pay attention to WHAT. Pay attention to what energizes you and what doesn't. Also pay attention to what is working and what isn't and why.

Consider WHO. Take inventory of the company you keep. With whom do you surround yourself? Are the people around you supportive, honest, and positive, or do they impact your life in neutral or even negative ways? Avoid or minimize interacting with "energy vampires"—people whose negativity drains your energy.

Describe WHERE you want to be. Can you describe your desired state? What does it look like, what are you doing, who is there with you, how does it feel?

Have a compelling WHY. Get clear on WHY you want what you want. What will it bring you? What will you experience and how will it make you feel? What will fulfill you?

Mind your mind-set. Your state of mind is one of the most important considerations. Are you thinking positively? Are you focusing on all that is right and good while working with others and yourself? Cultivate a healthy mind-set by managing your thoughts and words, as they will influence your actions and outcomes.

Embrace your suck. Are you perfectionistic, overly critical of yourself and others, complaining, whining, on a guilt trip, a martyr, or stuck in a victim mind-set? Yikes! Remember to *embrace your suck*. Accept it, rather than try to beat yourself up or fix all your shortcomings. Focus more on aligning and developing your natural talents, strengths, and interests, and do the same with others.

Understand, align, and leverage yourself and others. Remember, we are not all the same. Respect, celebrate, and leverage these differences.

Be accountable and hold others accountable. Establish and manage agreements with yourself and others. Your credibility and effectiveness, and theirs, depend on it.

Be grateful. Choosing to think positively and live gratefully are perhaps the most influential factors for living a happy life, as you work your ASSets off.

conclusion

WE ARE ALL BORN WITH INHERENT ABILITIES. When we create or place ourselves in an environment that allows us to act primarily from our strengths, we are most fulfilled. While we can all improve in different areas, and acquire or develop additional skills, it takes an extraordinary amount of effort and time to do something *well* that doesn't naturally suit us.

You will achieve better results and experience greater satisfaction by doing things that align with your natural talents, gifts, abilities, and interests. So instead of feeling frustrated and spending extra time and energy working harder than necessary, shift your paradigm to working your ASSets off.

Now get out there! Start working your ASSets off and live a more fulfilled life!

> *"You don't have to be great to start,*
> *but you have to start to be great."*
> —Zig Ziglar

12 Truths to Help You Work Your ASSets Off

1. Working Your ASSets Off—Not Working Hard—Leads to Success

2. It's Better to Be Great at Being You Than to Be Good at Everything

3. The "F" Word—Focus—It Is Essential to <u>F</u>ocus <u>O</u>n <u>C</u>ultivating <u>U</u>nique <u>S</u>trengths

4. People Want to Be Treated How *They* Want to Be Treated, Not the Way *You* Want to Be Treated

5. People Are Hired Because of Their Skills but Fired for Not Being Liked

6. ShiFt Happens When You Leverage Your Team's Strengths

7. It Is Important to Know What's Working and What's Not

8. HOW Is Easy When You Know Your WHY

9. Your Network Is One of Your Most Valuable ASSets

10. You Create Your Own Results

11. Gratitude Is the Gateway to Happiness

12. Get Your ASSets to Work, and You'll Live Your Best Life!

ABOUT THE AUTHOR

Allison Tabor

The owner of Coppia Advisory, a successful executive coaching and consulting business, Allison helps business owners, executives, and their teams in the areas of leadership, interpersonal communication, and strategic planning.

Allison also facilitates for the international Women Presidents' Organization (WPO), leading two peer advisory groups of San Francisco Bay Area women presidents and CEOs of multimillion-dollar companies. Additionally, she is a group leader for ProVisors, a community of professionals who serve their clients as trusted advisors and share the highest standards of integrity, performance, and accountability.

Prior to running her coaching and consulting business, Allison co-owned and led a successful structural engineering company with her husband for twenty-three years. She is certified as a DISC Consultant, One Page Business Plan® Specialist, and Professional Coach. With her love of business and behavioral science, Allison is a Master Connector who seeks to understand and help people reach their full potential. She has made a difference with hundreds of business owners and executives in a wide range of industries including professional services, manufacturing, retail, construction, and hospitality. Many of the businesses she's coached are family owned.

Born in Queens, New York, Allison loves living in the Bay Area with her husband of thirty-plus years and young adult daughter. She enjoys ballroom dancing—one place where she isn't a leader!

author photo by Lara George

Storyzon is a California-based publisher of business-oriented books as well as custom-tailored personal and corporate histories. True to its commitment to chronicle the breadth and beauty of life in its many forms, Storyzon donates a part of its proceeds to the preservation of inspiring stories of individuals without means.

STORYZON LLC, SAN FRANCISCO, CA
WWW.STORYZON.COM